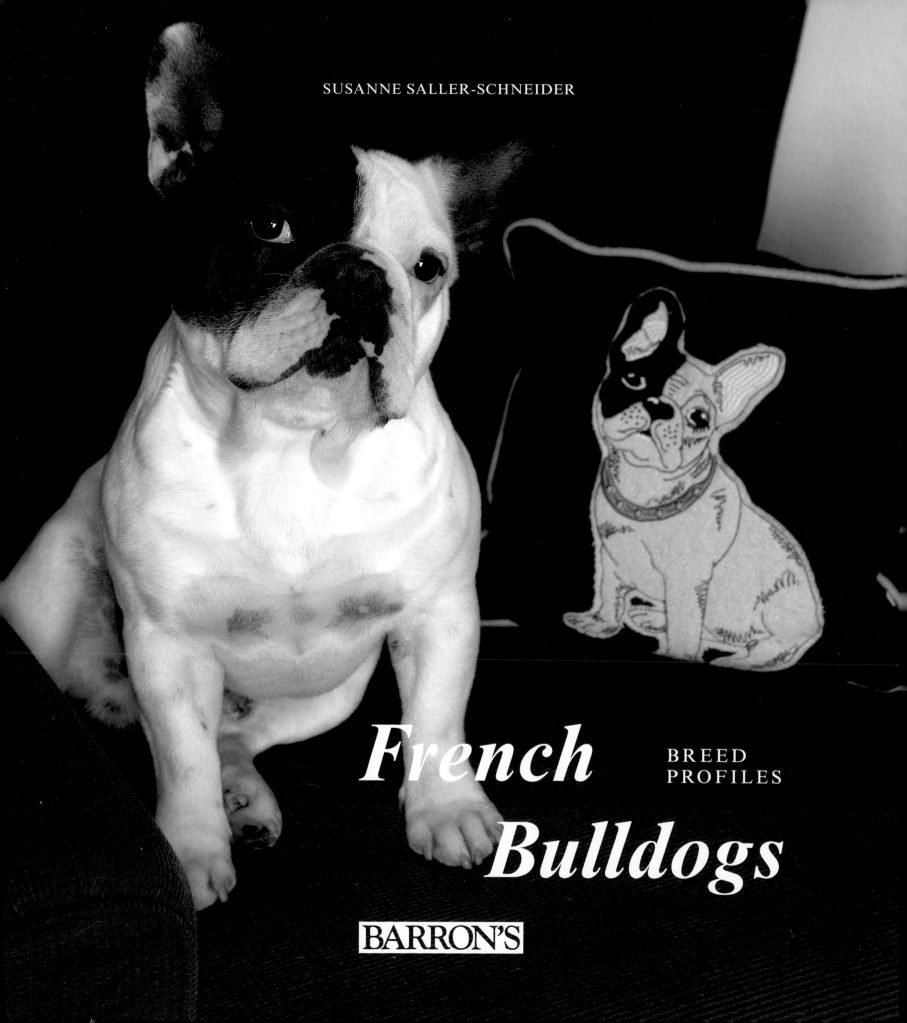

SUSANNE SALLER-SCHNEIDER

French **BREED PROFILES**

Bulldogs

BARRON'S

French Bulldogs

SUSANNE SALLER-SCHNEIDER

Contents

MY HEART BELONGS TO FAT, LITTLE DOGS

I think my passion for dogs came to me in the cradle. When I was a child, my parents gave me an Irish Setter—a great playmate that was soon joined by a Longhaired Dachshund. Many years later, well into my adulthood, I longed for another four-legged companion. That's how I got my first French Bulldog. At some point I got an urge to have another Frenchy. I wanted a female so that one day some charming little puppies would see the light of day. So Daphne von der Pleissenaue became my breeding female. I know one thing for sure: I certainly will have French Bulldogs as long as I live—and who knows, maybe my daughter Linda will also share my passion one day.

Susanne Saller-Schneider has been living with French Bulldogs since the mid-1990s. She is the second president of the International French Bulldog Club and the first chairperson of the regional committee for Bavaria, Germany. In 2005 she founded her regulation kennel, named Von der Rothenberg-Festung. Currently her (canine) family consists of three French Bulldogs and one elderly female Pug.

Susanne Saller-Schneider

FRENCH BULLDOGS

Snub nose, wide eyes, big ears—with their comical, crinkly faces, Frenchies have some of the most striking features in the dog world. Anyone who has taken these little hooligans to heart will be smitten for a lifetime.

Origin and History

It is perhaps surprising that a dog as cute as the French Bulldog is descended from huge Molossers. In antiquity these feared fighting dogs easily stood more than 31 inches (80 cm) high at the shoulder and weighed 220 pounds (100 kg). Like nearly all present-day dogs, though, Frenchies are the product of crossing various breeds, so we know where and when the first Frenchy-type dogs appeared, and that they have the same ancestors as their English relatives. The precise origin of the breed is not certain, however. There's just one thing for sure: the country of origin of these exceptionally charming dogs, which continually find increasing numbers of enthusiastic devotees, is France.

Which was there first: the dog or the pillow?

English Bulldog, with the breed-typical bat ears that quickly won the heart of many dog lovers.

A Briton in Paris

As a result of the English economic crisis at the end of the nineteenth century, countless workers were forced to leave the island. They sought their fortune in Normandy. They brought the little dogs along; because of their size, they were ideal for the living conditions in the working-class and poor districts.

As a hobby and in order to boost the family income, the English emigrants bred their toy Bulldogs. They were successful, for these English dogs represented a piece of the old country for the guest workers.

The breeders were not too selective in choosing mates. They mixed in Pugs, Griffons, various Terriers, and their mongrel offspring, and thus they had a major influence on the appearance and the disposition of today's breed. When the appearance changed, so did the name of the breed. At first the small dogs with the solid, muscular bone structure were called Terrier-Boules. Visually they sometimes strongly resembled today's French Bulldog, especially when an animal had erect ears, as was the case with increasing frequency, instead of the rose ears that were more common in Bulldogs.

The First Clubs

The Terrier-Boules had already conquered Paris by 1880 when a group of breeders and aficiona-

13

More than 100 years ago contributions from breeders and dog lovers from many countries ensured that we can enjoy these beautiful little, agile dogs today.

The French Bulldog found many devotees in America's upper class, as this engraving from the 1920s shows.

dos in the capital launched the club Les Amants des Terrier-Boules; in weekly meetings they enthusiastically exchanged information about the beloved breed. In 1885 the Club Amical compiled the first tentative breed registry. Since the breed's popularity continued to increase, in 1888 the French Bulldog Club (Club du Bouledogue Français) was founded. But it took 10 more years for the Société Centrale de Canine (an amalgamation of purebred dog clubs) to take the breeding seriously and establish its own club for French Bulldog fans. At the urging of the Société Centrale de Canine both clubs eventually merged under the name Club Bouledogue France.

The cute little Bulldogs quickly found many devotees in France and soon were positively "à la mode." No longer did they accompany only freighters, butchers, and coachmen in their daily work. More and more ladies and gentlemen of the highest Parisian society found pleasure in the dogs' extravagant appearance and lovable disposition. Contemporary artists such as Henri de Toulouse-Lautrec were just as fascinated with the friendly creatures as the "upper crust." Even the English king Edward VII and the last Russian czarist family owned French Bulldogs.

The "Frenchy" Conquers England

In 1893 when a British dog judge turned up at the most famous dog show in the country—the Kennel Club Show—with six freshly imported French Bulldogs and showed them in the light Bulldog class, it was a complete sensation. The spectators marveled at the elegant little dogs with the big, erect ears; their attentive disposition and their agility made a great impression. Everywhere people spoke and wrote about the charming creatures from Paris. No wonder the Frenchies stole the show from the English Toy Bulldogs in the truest sense of the word. We can imagine the unfriendly and hostile reaction to the intruders on the part of the old, established English breeders. Ultimately they felt that there should be no Bulldogs other than the English. An angry toy Bulldog breeder wrote in the *Kennel Gazette*, "It is nothing more than the rebirth of our Toys. But it cannot be said that the layover in Paris has benefited it. Aside from a perfect French accent and impeccable manners they have contributed nothing but flaws, for example those hideous bat ears."

Because they didn't know how else to react, the disgruntled British Toy breeders eventually demanded that the new Bulldogs be designated as an English breed rather than a French one. In the end it could not be denied that they were descended from the English Toys. But neither the French breeders nor the English judges agreed with this claim—and after some flip-flopping, the judges won the dispute over the name: The French Bulldog remained French.

Real Frenchy devotees search for old, original collectors' pieces relative to their favorite animal in every antiques shop and every flea market.

In England, where the Bulldog Club at first was in charge of both French Bulldogs and Toy Bulldogs, the disputes over the breed's origin and designation dragged on. In 1906 the English Kennel Club finally stepped in and as the highest authority forbade mixing the two breeds. This decision meant the end of the Toys, for the number of their devotees quickly fell, to the advantage of the French Bulldogs. By 1930 the breed had eventually disappeared slowly but completely.

Frenchies all over the World—
USA and Europe

The English and the French are not the only ones who played an important role in the development of the French Bulldog, for the Americans also contributed a great deal. In contrast to England, the new breed was given an enthusiastic reception in the United States. As early as 1896 American Georges Phelps went to Paris to seek particularly exemplary specimens of the breed that had captivated him during his trip to Europe at the end of the 1880s: the French Bulldog. With the support of an English veterinarian who was working at the Paris Dog Show, and thanks to his own persistence and a certain amount of luck, Phelps eventually was able to acquire two particularly beautiful dogs with bat ears. They were to provide the cornerstone for Frenchy breeding in the United States. On that side of the Atlantic was the upper crust in particular that took interest in the little dogs. Demand was strong, and soon

Without question, the similarity cannot be denied. That may be why many Boxer owners also have a Frenchy.

enthusiastic American Frenchy fans were traveling to Paris to buy an authentic puppy.

The significant influences in the development of the breed surely came from England, France, and North America. Yet its history cannot be separated from the initial breeding in Austria, Germany, and Switzerland.

First, in Germany, Max Hartenstein dedicated himself to breeding French Bulldogs. The famous dog breeder had become acquainted with the breed as early as 1870 during a trip to France, and he imported from Paris some outstanding specimens for his kennel, called Plavia, in Berlin. In southern Germany the Austrian-born Marianne Mueller dominated French Bulldog breeding at the kennel named von der

Mühle in Gräfeling, near Munich. Berlin and Munich thus quickly became the centers of German Frenchy breeding. Breeding in Austria and Switzerland began around 1890, just a few years after the start of official breeding in France.

Early History and French Bulldog Clubs

In 1909 Frenchy enthusiasts from four countries came together in Munich—they included the Spaniard John Blacker, the Germans Heinrich Knotz and Max Hartenstein, the Englishman Ernest Langford, and the Austrian Marianne Müller—to found the Internationale Bouledogue Français-Club (IBFC). In Germany this first German Frenchy club still exists under the name of Internationaler Klub Französischer Buldoggen (IKFB). The association's first official breed book was published in 1913. It registered 306 French Bulldogs in Germany, from a total of 58 kennels.

In the same year Hartenstein won all first places at the Paris Dog Show with his dogs. The male Patrice Plavia even won the title Best of Breed among 120 French Bulldogs at the show. Based on this tremendous success, Hartenstein's kennel exerted great influence on breeding in the entire German-speaking region.

There is also a French Bulldog Club of America; it was founded in 1897, and is the world's oldest club dedicated to this breed.

The Future of Breeding

In recent years the number of Frenchy breeders and litters has increased dramatically. On average 320 pups are entered into the breed book every year. These exceptional dogs are continually turning up more devotees.

Because of its short snout, the French Bulldog has come under increasing scrutiny by animal protection advocates in Europe worried about defective breeding, so the IKFB set the breeding requirements even higher than before. Now, a potential breeding animal must be able to cover a little more than a half mile (1 km) within 10 minutes so that its conditioning can be evaluated, the heart rate after exertion can be checked, and it can be determined whether the dog has breathing difficulties.

In addition, it has become mandatory to examine breeding animals using the most recent medical tests for hereditary defects and other diseases. An X-ray of the spinal column and a close inspection of the patella (kneecap) are likewise compulsory tests, to prevent ailments in offspring to the extent possible. The aim of future breeding must be healthy Frenchies true to the breed.

None of these requirements is currently in force in the United States, however.

English King Edward VII was also a Frenchy enthusiast. He helped raise the breed to great popularity in his homeland.

Related Breeds

No question about it: the French Bulldog is really unique. This is not just because the breeders in the nineteenth century mixed a wide variety of dog breeds—including the four-legged "relatives" shown here, which still influence the Frenchy's typical appearance.

PUG

The Frenchy gets its square, compact physical appearance (lots of mass in a small space) from small mastifflike comrades.

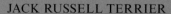

JACK RUSSELL TERRIER

Outwardly this breed is less similar to the Frenchy than some others, such as the Pug. But the small, powerful, lively working terrier is responsible for the agility of today's Frenchies.

BRUSSELS GRIFFON

These little Belgians are intelligent and alert—and it's precisely this characteristic that they have passed on to the Frenchy. Another similarity: both breeds occasionally have nearly humanlike facial expressions.

FRENCH MASTIFF/BORDEAUX BULLDOG

This dog is among the largest relatives: the Molossers. As with the Frenchy, the coat is short and smooth, the body muscular and athletic. Like the French Bulldog, it is not a barker and has a sensitive disposition.

TYPICAL FRENCHY–*From their physical characteristics it is easy to recognize who the dogs' ancestors are. You can see that they come from good parentage.*

BULLDOG

The common ancestors are hard to miss: like their English relatives, today's Frenchies are broad, stocky, and low to the ground. But they are smaller, smaller boned, and much lighter.

The Breed Today

Clown, philosopher, aristocrat, charmer, a small dog with the brave heart of a lion: all these attempts to describe the French Bulldog's character are as varied as they are accurate. Neither the bat ears nor the tail are clipped. The coat is not trimmed, but naturally smooth and short. As unusual as the French Bulldog appears, everything is genuine. Its friendly character, its good disposition, and its joie de vivre make it a wonderful companion for every dog lover. Frenchies do one thing best: captivate people from the first glance and spark a great and everlasting love.

What Frenchies Are Like

French Bulldogs polarize people. Some just can't warm up to the breed; others fall for it head over heels. This surely is because of their unconventional appearance.

The French Bulldog certainly has experienced a major boom in recent years. For a long time a Frenchy puppy in a dog-training school was considered exotic, but nowadays in many places you can find plenty of short-nosed company.

Since there is often a demand for the uncommon, French Bulldogs have recently turned increasingly into fashionable dogs. More and more people adorn themselves with this idiosyncratic, muscular, and elegant purebred dog.

Since the dogs' health is all too often sacrificed to uncontrolled mass breeding and a quick profit, a fashion-dog trend can cause great harm to a breed. As a Frenchy fan or future owner you should always keep the Frenchy's specific needs in mind and get information about breeders and breeding before you buy a puppy.

What Frenchies Are Like—Character, Characteristics, and Needs
In contrast to many other small dog breeds, the Frenchy is no barker, but rather a calm dog. With adequate exercise it can be kept successfully indoors. But it should not have to climb too many steps, because this is harmful to its spinal column.

Hardly anything gets by its curiosity and alertness, despite its calm nature; however, it is not suited to protection or herding duty, and hunting with French Bulldogs is also decidedly not recommended. As the outward appearance indicates, the little dogs are also not born athletes, so if you are looking for a dog that will accompany you on long bicycling or jogging forays, it would be better to steer clear of this breed.

The Frenchy does love long walks through field, forest, and meadow; sometimes it can also sprint like a Greyhound, and when it plays, it tends toward exuberance. But it is not a high-performance endurance athlete, and this is partly because of its shortness of breath.

The French Bulldog is also not a keen lapdog. Granted, it likes its naps on the couch and loafing around for hours—and as with Pugs, its sleep is often accompanied by grunting, snoring, and slurping noises at every pitch imaginable. But the dog's daily routine should not be too sedentary. Even the most placid dog can develop bad habits and disagreeable quirks if it becomes bored or has too little to do.

A Tender Soul in a Rough Shell
French Bulldogs are simply friendly little companion dogs. What they love best is to be around their humans and to take part in everyday living. The worst misery for a Frenchy is being left alone in the house or a crate for hours. More than many other breeds, the dog needs and seeks closeness to its master or mistress. It longs to be petted and will gladly let people ruffle its coat, preferably for hours, and then fall asleep peacefully while grunting. Without this attention it would atrophy emotionally.

Ultimately the Frenchy is a faithful, loving companion that wholeheartedly bestows its love on its master, mistress, or family—and wants to please. So if you settle on a French Bulldog, you will have a true companion that will stick by your side in any situation.

A certain amount of training is still necessary with a small dog so that daily things like going for a walk don't turn into a running of the gauntlet.

A Little Hardhead

Naturally, you can go through the companion dog test at any time with a Frenchy. Still, nearly every Frenchy owner probably will make the sobering discovery that these dogs really have their own will—and, for example, would rather soak up the sunshine than train.

A French Bulldog is not a working dog that immediately does everything you want, even if it is thoroughly docile. Once the little Molosser gets something into its little round head, it's hard to undo it. This stubbornness should not be underestimated; a French Bulldog has character. In many everyday situations it tends to overestimate itself and refuses to be intimidated even by bigger dogs. But it is never vicious or aggressive.

What you see here is a real Frenchy dynasty: great-grandma Daffy, mother Emma, daughter Anea (from left to right), and, in front, great-grandson Schecki. Beauty and class are indeed hereditary.

Many Frenchy owners whose dogs are related know each other personally. The advantage to this is that the breeders are very well informed about the individual breeding animals: they not only see them in the show ring, but also know how they behave in their accustomed surroundings. That way they have lots more information about the dogs' disposition, which in turn is an advantage in breeding.

My Story

At home she has a big dog that many children would envy. But her heart belongs to her grandparents' two saucy Frenchies. At first Louise was as unenthusiastic as her brother Albert over the fact that Grandma and Grandpa were going to have more puppies. Then after the death of their Rottweiler mix, they finally had time to go to the playground with them.

Who's comforting whom here? Children who grow up with dogs know that they will always have a trusted friend at their side.

The first time I saw Molly and Filou, I thought that our grandparents had bought us two guinea pigs. Since our own dog is huge, I never would have thought that a puppy could be so tiny. Of course my little brother and I immediately started playing with the two of them and cuddling them—and we thought they were much better than guinea pigs. Molly and Filou couldn't keep it up very long, though, so they crawled back together to sleep in their little bed. At that time they were really babies. But they both grew pretty quickly and turned really saucy. We now had to be careful when we were playing because their baby teeth were really sharp. At that time Albert was just two years old, and he often stumbled when he ran. Of course Molly and Filou made the most of that.

My parents and granddad scolded the dogs from time to time. Now Molly and Filou are almost 4 years old. So they could be a mom and dad themselves. But they are from the same litter, and besides, Molly is spayed. Now we can take Molly and Filou for walks all by ourselves because they don't pull hard on the leash or run away. Molly doesn't like cats; if she sees one while we're on a walk, we have to be careful that she doesn't run away and chase after it, because

we don't really know if she would find her way back home. She might also run into the street.

Playing with Molly and Filou is great. They aren't too strong, and we don't have to watch out for wagging tails, like with our own dog. When he is happy, he can really hurt someone. Also Molly and Filou don't slobber all over like our dog does.

What we love best is throwing balls for the two dogs or teaching them little tricks. That doesn't work too well yet, but it will. They're both greedy little pigs anyway, and that will only get worse with more treats. Maybe then we can put on a real circus performance for Grandma and Grandpa. I would never put a short, pink skirt on Molly, because I think that's cruelty to animals.

We each have our favorite dog. That works out because we don't have to argue so much and each dog gets the same amount of petting. My brother Albert likes Filou more, and I like Molly. When I am sad, she comes over to me and comforts me. She hops onto the couch, puts her paw on my leg, and looks at me with her big wide eyes. Then I can tell her everything that's making me sad or angry. She keeps all secrets to herself. So I am always happy when we see each other again.

True love: for Louise there is nothing better than romping in the yard and cuddling with Molly.

LOUISE (10) AND HER BROTHER ALBERT (6) are growing up with three dogs. While a good-natured old Great Dane snoozes the day away at home, they can romp around to their hearts' content with their grandparents' French Bulldogs, Molly and Filou.

The FCI/AKC Standard

As the largest umbrella organization for dogs, the Fédération Cynologique Internationale (FCI for short) supports the breeding and utilization of purebred dogs worldwide. Its member and partner countries organize international dog shows, train breeding and performance judges, and issue pedigrees. In North America, the American Kennel Club (AKC) and the Canadian Kennel Club perform a similar function.

One of the duties of the major dog associations is to publish valid breed standards. These specify what the ideal appearance of a breed should be and which characteristics are desirable. The focus is less on the dogs' well-being: health, disposition, and behavior are generally not at the top of the list.

The FCI French Bulldog breed standard is very similar to that of the American Kennel Club (AKC) and other U.S. breed clubs' standard, and covers all Frenchy features. When an American owner is planning to show or breed Frenchies, though, he or she should consult the AKC standard, which is found on its web site and in the *AKC Complete Dog Book*.

The Breed Standard for French Bulldogs
As early as 1898, the same year in which the Société Centrale de Canine recognized the French Bulldog as a breed, there was a breed standard; it was revised and edited in 1931–32, 1948, and 1986. Today's breed standard, which is valid for all FCI member countries, has been in force since 1995.

GENERAL APPEARANCE
The French Bulldog is a typical, small-sized Molosser. Despite its small size, it is a powerful, generally short, and compact dog with a short coat, a short, snub-nose face, protruding ears, and naturally short tail. It must communicate the impression of being a lively, alert, very muscular animal of compact structure and solid bone structure.

BEHAVIOR AND CHARACTER
Good-natured, happy, playful, athletic, cheerful nature. Particularly loving around its owners and with children.

HEAD
The head must be very powerful, broad, and square: the skin covering it forms nearly symmetrical folds and wrinkles. The head is distinguished by a receding upper jaw and nose area: the skull makes up for its reduced length with breadth.

TOP OF THE HEAD
Skull: broad, nearly flat, with strongly arched forehead. The prominent eyebrow arches are separated by a particularly well-developed furrow between the eyes. The furrow must not continue onto the forehead. Very underdeveloped occipital crest. The stop is very noticeable.

FACIAL BONES
Nose: broad, very short and raised; nostrils are open and symmetrical, and tilted rearward. But the inclination of the nostrils and the raised (upturned) nose must allow for normal breathing.

Top of muzzle: very short and broad: exhibits concentric, symmetrical folds running down to the upper flews (length: a sixth of the total head length).

Flews: thick, somewhat flaccid and black; the upper flews meet the lower in the middle and

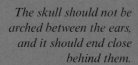

The skull should not be arched between the ears, and it should end close behind them.

cover the teeth completely (the teeth must not be visible). In profile the upper flew droops and is rounded. The tongue must not be visible.

Jaw: broad, square, and powerful. The lower jaw forms a broad arch and ends in front of the upper jaw. With the muzzle closed the arched shape of the lower jaw moderates the protrusion of the lower jaw (undershot bite). The arched shape is necessary to avoid excessive protrusion of the lower jaw.

Teeth: The incisors on the lower jaw must in no case fall behind the upper incisors. The lower dental arch is rounded. The jaws must not be displaced laterally or contorted. The distance between the dental arches cannot be stipulated precisely: upper flew and lower flew must meet

each other in such a way that the teeth are fully covered.

Jowls: The jowl musculature is well developed, but not bulging.

Eyes: alert expression; deeply set eye, quite far from the nose and especially from the ears; dark in color, rather large, nice and round, slightly protruding, and with no trace of white (white uvea) when the animal looks straight ahead. The edge of the eyelid must be black.

Ears: medium large, broad at the base and rounded at the top. They are set high on the head, but without being too close to each other and are carried erect. The external ear is open toward the front. The skin must be thin and must feel soft.

No one will upstage this young brindle male very easily: His legs are straight, and the shoulders are short, thick, and firmly muscled. The upper arm is short, and the elbows are in contact with the body. The forefeet are powerful and short. It all adds up to a really fine specimen.

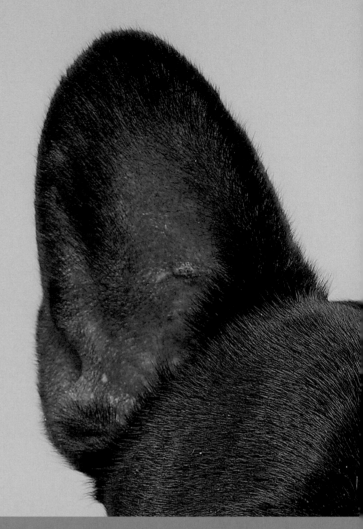

The dark eyes are quite large, handsome, and round, and they protrude slightly. When the animal is looking straight ahead, no white is visible. The edge of the eyelid must be black.

The bat ears are medium-large and rounded at the top. They sit high on the head and are carried erect. The external ear is open toward the front.

THROAT
Short, slightly arched, with no dewlap

BODY
Topline: rises consistently to the lumbar region and then drops quickly to the tail. Reason for the desired shape: the short haunch.

Back: broad and muscular

Loin: short and broad

Croup: inclined

Chest: cylindrical and very deep: barrel-shaped, strong, rounded ribs

Forechest: broad and open

Lower profile line and belly: tucked up, but not Greyhoundlike

TAIL
Short, low on the croup and adjoining the buttocks, thick at the base; or skewed tail; tapered at the tip. Even in movement it must remain below horizontal. A relatively long, tapering, skewed tail that does not reach as far as the plane of the hock joint is permissible but not desirable.

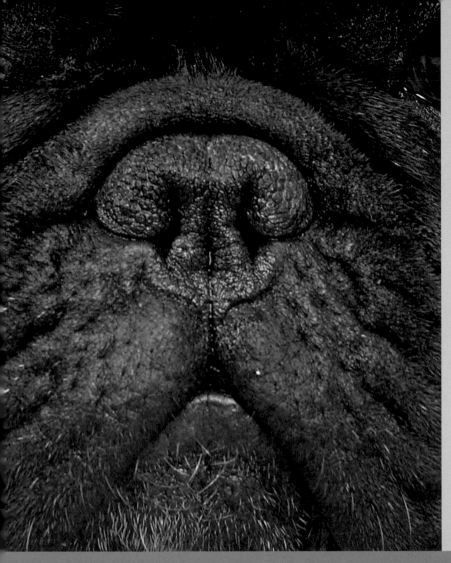

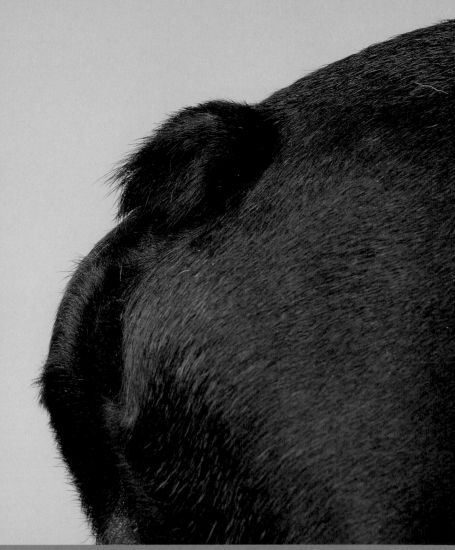

The nostrils are well opened and symmetrical. The inclination of the nostrils and the upturned nose must permit normal breathing.

The short tail is thick at the base and placed low on the croup. It contacts the buttocks and has at least two vertebrae. When it wags, it must remain below horizontal.

LIMBS
Forequarters: straight and vertical when viewed from both the side and the front

Shoulders: short, thick; protruding, firm musculature

Upper arm: short

Elbow: must contact the body

Lower arm: short, well articulated, straight, and muscular

Carpus/Pastern: powerful and short

Hindquarters: The rear legs are powerful and muscular; they are slightly longer than the front legs and thus raise the hindquarters. They are straight and vertical when viewed from the side and the rear.

Upper thigh: muscular, firm, not too rounded

Hock: positioned low, not too angled, but especially not too steep

Rear pastern: powerful and short. From birth the French Bulldog may have no dewclaws.

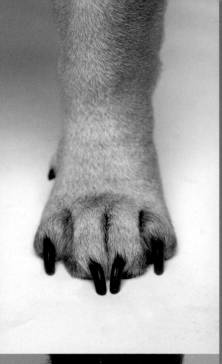

Since the paws are so round and small, they are also called cat feet. The toes are compact, the pads hard, thick, and black. On brindle Frenchies the short, thick nails must be black. With all other colors dark nails are preferred.

Paws: The front paws are round and small ("cat feet"): good contact with the ground, turned slightly outward. The toes are very compact, the claws short, thick, and well off-set. The pads are hard, thick, and black. With brindle animals the claws must be black. Dark nails are preferred with fawn brindle dogs with intermediate white spotting and dun-colored dogs with intermediate or prevalent white spotting, but there is no penalty for light-colored nails. The rear paws are very compact.

GAIT

The motion sequence is free: the legs move parallel to the median plane of the body.

COAT

Hair: attractive, thick, gleaming and soft, short hair

Color: even fawn, brindle, or non-brindled fawn with intermediate or prevalent spotting

All gradations of tan are permissible, from "red" to "latte." Completely white dogs are assigned the color "brindled fawn with prevalent white spotting." With particularly beautiful dogs with very dark nose and dark eyes and dark eyelid rims, a certain depigmentation in the face is tolerated as an exception.

SIZE AND WEIGHT

A French Bulldog in good condition must not weigh less than 17.6 pounds (8 kg) and not more than 30.8 pounds (14 kg), and the size must be in proportion to the weight.

Flaws

At dog shows every deviation from the following points is considered a flaw, which should be weighted with respect to the degree of deviation. Many anatomical deviations can lead to health problems, such as closed nostrils (stenotic nares).

- tight or narrowed nose, chronic snorer
- failure of flews to close at the front (the lips do not close)
- light-colored eyes
- dewlap (hanging skin folds on the throat)
- tail carried high; too long or abnormally short tail
- loose elbows (elbows turned outward to a degree)
- hock too steep or displaced forward (no angling in the hindquarters)
- incorrect gait (all gaits that deviate substantially from a parallel gait)
- spotted coat
- excessively long hair

Major Flaws

- visible incisors when the mouth is closed
- visible tongue when mouth is closed
- "drumming" dog (quick movement of forelegs)
- depigmented areas on the face, except for fawn brindle dogs with occasional white spotting and fawn-colored dogs with intermediate or prevalent white spotting ("fawn")
- excessive or insufficient weight (no less than 17.6 or more than 30.8 pounds [8–14 kg]

- the lower incisors close behind the upper
- canine teeth always visible with mouth closed
- different-colored eyes
- ears are not carried upright
- ears, tail, or dewclaws clipped
- dewclaws on the rear limbs removed or present
- no tail
- hair color of "black and tan," "mouse," or "brown"

Disqualifying Flaws

- clear physical abnormalities
- nose of some color other than black
- harelip

Postscript

Male dogs must display two normally developed testicles completely contained in the scrotum; otherwise, the dog is flawed.

The French Bulldog's coat is thick, shiny, and soft—even without lots of care. The dog sheds significantly only when it changes coat in the spring and fall.

*Dark, large, round eyes with
pigmented eyelid rim*

*Large, symmetrical nostrils;
short, broad top of muzzle*

*Broad, square, powerful jaw: the
lower row of teeth must not be
behind the upper incisors (overbite)*

*Square, powerful, broad head
with even fold formation*

*Slightly arched, short
throat with no dewlap*

The FCI/AKC Standards at a Glance

*Straight, vertical forelegs.
Paws turned outward,
elbows close to the body.*

Bat ears high on head and carried erect, with rounded tips

Broad, muscular back (roach-backed)

Short tail low on the croup; must lie on the buttocks

Muscular, straight, vertical hind legs. The hock must be neither too steep nor too bent.

Cylindrical, very deep chest

Small, round paws (cat feet). The color of the nails corresponds to the hair color.

Color Variants

No sooner do you decide on a French Bulldog than the next question comes up: what color should the dog be? A pied (or piebald) certainly is very attractive and a good deal more striking than a dark Frenchy. But even a fawn-colored French Bulldog with a handsome black face mask is a wonderful sight. As it so often happens, beauty is in the eye of the beholder—and sometimes fashion plays a role. Until a few years ago, dark brindle Frenchies were most common in Europe. Pied bulldogs were quite a rarity, and fawn-colored animals weren't yet even entered in dog shows. In some places, fawn-colored dogs were long excluded from breeding, so this color was scarcely to be seen. In some countries (e.g., the Netherlands, Belgium, and France), the situation was different. More and more fawn-colored Frenchies were born—and so this color now enriches the palette of the various coats, which does not exactly make decisions any easier for future owners. In the United States, fawn is the most common color as well as the most popular at shows. On the following pages, you will find an overview of the various colors and their most important features.

Colors of the French Bulldog

In some places, only dark brindle, dun-colored, and pied dogs in a wide variety are allowed to breed. Serious breeders therefore offer no other colors. Regardless of the color, a French Bulldog's coat must be very thick and shiny.

It's the mix that matters: both of these Frenchies are pieds, but the one on the left has fawn-colored patches, and the one on the right has brindle markings. With both variants, good black pigmentation on the nose, lips, and eyes is important.

For a long time there were only dark-colored Frenchies in Europe. It took until 1995, with the revision of the breed standards there, for fawn-colored dogs to gain approval for breeding and showing. The previously very exceptional coat color gained quick acceptance, and selective breeding (especially with animals from other countries) successfully increased the new "fashion color." The situation in the United States was somewhat different, with fawn-colored dogs generally being in greater favor.

The demand for fawn-colored Bulldogs was huge in the first few years—and that entailed some consequences. On the one hand, many breeders demanded exorbitant prices for the (still) rare coat color. On the other, the dog's appearance also suffered. At first, people were mindful of a black mask (the face should appear nicely defined in black) and dark nails, but then there were more and more dogs with light-colored nails. Small beauty defects such as inadequate pigmentation in the dark eyelids and the lips also became more common. Even if you have your heart set on a certain color, the dog's health must be far more important than the mere visual effect—caution is advised in dealing with "fashion colors."

Color Definition

The official standard describes the colors of the French Bulldog as follows: "Even fawn, brindle or non-brindle, or with defined spotting. Brindle or non-brindle fawn with moderate or prevalent spotting. All gradations of coat color are permissible, from red through latte. Completely white dogs are assigned the color brindle fawn with prevalent white spotting. When a dog displays a very dark nose and dark eyes with dark eyelid rims, with particularly handsome specimens a certain depigmentation in the face may be tolerated as an exception."

In a nutshell, the basic color of all French Bulldogs is fawn, or a warm beige. For example, the basic color of a Frenchy colloquially referred to as a dark brindle is thus not black

with golden brindle markings; this is more correctly a fawn-colored Bulldog with dark brindle.

Brindle Frenchies

As explained above, this involves a fawn-colored dog with dark brindle (a brownish or fawny hue with streaks of other colors). Most animals are not totally brindle, but have a more or less large white bib. With this coloration a distinction is generally made between dark and light brindle dogs. This refers not to the color, but rather to the intensity of the brindle: a dark brindle fawn-colored French Bulldog has intense brindle, and a light brindle fawn-colored dog has only a little brindle. Nails, lips, nose, and eyelids should always be dark.

White and Brindle (Pied) Frenchies

As with the brindle Frenchy, with the white and brindle the base color is fawn, even if the coat appears predominantly white. The dun-colored spots in the coat should be brindle. Fairly large black spots (as with Dalmatians) are not desirable, and yet dogs of this type can be bred. However, Dalmatian spots are not to be confused with pigmentation spots; the latter refers not to hair color, but rather to dark pigment spots in the skin.

The White Frenchy

Interestingly, even the pure white dogs are considered to be pied. Basically these animals generally are not what their appearance suggests:

These three coat colors have existed only since 1998. They are the fawn-colored Frenchy (even fawn with defined spots), the fawn-pied (even fawn with prevalent spotting), and the Frenchy with the very light fawn base color.

Here you see five different pieds—and the palette is far from complete, for with every specimen Mother Nature introduces something new and unique. This is how every future Frenchy owner finds a dog. With all variants the black pigment on the nose, the lips, and the eyes is important.

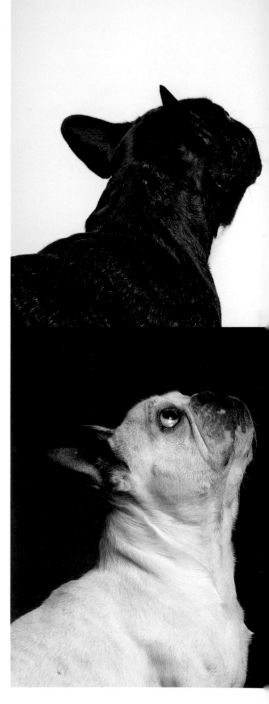

pure white. It's just that their white spots are very pronounced. The eyelids, nose, and lips of white Frenchies must be fully pigmented. Pigmented spots on the skin are easier to see with white Frenchies than with dark brindle dogs. In contrast to the undesirable Dalmatian spots this is not a flaw.

With brindles and especially with white Frenchies, dirty spots on the coat are more visible than with dark-colored dogs. To keep the hair looking beautiful in the long run, a shampoo for light-colored dog hair is recommended, like the ones used for West Highland White Terriers (another good bet: horse shampoo specifically for light-colored horses).

The Fawn (Dun-Colored) Frenchy

Fawn, the base color of all Frenchy color variants, is also a distinct color—and all shades from red to latte are permissible. The nails on fawns, like the pigmentation of the eyelids, nose, and lips, should be dark, and the mask should be black.

White and Fawn

With these dogs the white portion predominates over the fawn base color. The spots in the coat should be an even fawn color. The nails should be black, and the eyelids, nose, and lips fully pigmented.

Color Flaws

There are certain dog breeds in which the coat color of many animals is diluted and thus lightened. The recessive dilution gene is responsible for the color dilution; it controls the intensity of the coat color. If it is present in both sire and dam, the pigmentation storage in each individual hair clumps together and the color lightens. So, for example, with this tendency the coat of originally black dogs is designated as "blue" or "gray," and that of brown dogs as "lilac" or "Isabella." Diluted red hair is known as "apricot," and all light shades were diluted to "cream."

Health Consequences

Some blue dogs can have alopecia. No problems are observable in cream dogs.

Careful Selection of Breeding Animals

Usually breeders attempt to eliminate color flaws through selective breeding, and thus to protect the animals from health problems. Fortunately, through blood sampling it is very easy to determine with modern gene technology for DNA identification (parentage and hereditary traits) whether the breeding animals carry the dilution gene—and conscientious breeders are happy to use these new possibilities.

Care should be exercised in mating one pied with another. In puppies from this type of litter

A Frenchy like a harlequin: with brindle fawn accompanied by prevalent white spotting, the eyelids in the white area must be well pigmented.

This dog is designated in professional jargon as dark brindle, even fawn; but, according to the standard, it is called brindle with limited spotting (white marking on the chest).

it's not just that the eyelids, lips, and nose are not well pigmented. The young ones can also be born deaf, a phenomenon that occurs very frequently in Dalmatians. It is always advisable to mate a light-colored Frenchy with a dark brindle French Bulldog. Generally, there is also no problem in mating one dark brindle with another. Mouse, blue, chocolate-brown, and black dogs with brown markings (black and tan) are not allowed to breed in clubs that are part of the FCI. The same applies to French Bulldogs that are blue-brindle (from brindle) and blue-pied (from black-and-white pied).

Inadmissible Colors

Frenchies with wool-white to champagne-colored (cream) coats or pure black coats without any markings are also considered to have color flaws. But in contrast to the "blue" color flaw, dogs of this color are sometimes shown at dog shows.

Breed Standards in the United States

In the United States a different breed standard from that of the FCI applies. As early as 1925, the colors were prescribed as follows: "All colors are permissible—all brindle, fawn,

According to the standard, what laypeople would call "white hair" is a brindle fawn with predominant white spotting. In these cases, too, the eyelids should show as much pigmentation as possible.

A clearly defined black face mask is desirable in fawn-colored Frenchies. In this color, the nails should also be dark.

white, brindle and white, plus any other color, except for the inadmissible ones described in the following."

The disallowed colors include black and white, black and tan, liver (chocolate brown), mouse, and solid black (pure black without any brindle). As with the FCI, breeding with blue Frenchies is not recommended.

The cream color (in fact a lightened fawn variant) is allowed for breeding in the United States and is also presented at dog shows. The pedigree of imported dogs from the United States often includes cream-colored ancestors.

In practically every litter there is something for every taste. Males can pass on a variety of colors when they mate with a pied female. Then, in the same litter, there can also be dark brindle, fawn, and pied puppies.

Usually, the breeder has a good idea of the future color variations based on the choice of the parents. But as so often happens in life, sometimes things turn out other than expected, and we never know with total certainty what the puppies, which come into the world after about 63 days of gestation, will really look like. There's only one thing that can be said for sure: pure dark brindle strains occur very rarely. Mixed in somewhere there is almost always a pied Frenchy.

OUR FRENCHY

It takes many months for a clumsy puppy to turn into a fully grown little powerhouse.
Throughout this entire time the French Bulldog needs your complete devotion and love.
But you can be sure of this: it will all be returned to you.

A Frenchy It Is

Have you done some thorough research into a couple of breeds and after mature reflection decided that a wrinkle-nosed French Bulldog is the right choice for you? Have you geared up to organize your life around the needs of a little puppy, not just for the next few months but for many years? Then you are ready for your Frenchy.

But until the young dog actually moves in with you, there are still some things to take care of. First, you need to find a conscientious breeder who is planning to have a litter. And even if you know who to approach, you must be patient: with French Bulldogs, like all dogs, the gestation period lasts around two months, and then the puppies have to remain with their mother for at least nine weeks. Fortunately, nowadays, it is almost always possible to visit the new family member several times and create the first tender bonds.

How to Find a Conscientious Breeder

As a future dog owner, of course you want to choose a healthy puppy with a disposition that will suit you well. Ultimately, the pup will not just occupy a place in your life as a new family member, but will also be with you for a long time.

This puppy stares into the future with a curious gaze. What will his new home be like?

Most breeders love their dogs and give them exceptional care. But especially with dog breeds that experience a quick rise in popularity there are often people and dog retailers who try to do business with unregistered dogs. Before you buy a French Bulldog, you should determine whether the conditions that apply to serious breeders are being met.

Basically you should always make sure that the available puppies have registration papers. That is the only way to track the health of the previous generations and the offspring. In any case you should back away from a purchase in the following situations:

• Impulse buying without previous knowledge: with respected breeders the waiting list for a puppy is often long; in addition, conscientious breeders will want to find out about the new owners and the living conditions before handing over a puppy. Breeders who have no interest in the destination of their dogs will very rarely give their animals the necessary attention, and all they're interested in is a quick buck.

• The dam is not on the premises: only in the rarest of cases will you find both parent animals at the breeder's. Just to guarantee the health of the offspring the males come from other breeding lines. The females merely travel to be bred. But things are different with the puppies' mother: she must always live in the same household as the puppies. Always look at the dam and watch how she interacts with the puppies: Do they all appear to be intimately acquainted? Are the mother and puppies well nourished? Do the mother's teats indicate a recent birth?

• Unknown registration papers: if you are not sure about the papers presented, you should always take the time to research them thoroughly. Conscientious breeders should have no problem if you first want to get information from their clubs. They have nothing to conceal— on the contrary.

• A price for the puppy that is too high or too low: raising a litter of young dogs always requires significant work and involves high costs. This ranges from the stud fee for males to

The time with the mother is nearly up. This pup is old enough to go his own way.

the regular veterinary care for the pregnant and then nursing dam and the puppies. Pups that are offered for sale cheaply and below value are already short on basic care.

But you should also stay away from animals that are too expensive. Ultimately, in dog breeding, the healthy preservation of the breed must be the main consideration, and not profit. Neither a specific coat color nor the pedigree justifies an excessively high purchase price.

The web site of the recognized breed association can provide guidelines on appropriate prices.

• Puppies from many different breeds or an excessive number of dogs of one breed: as mentioned earlier, raising young dogs conscien-

tiously is an intensive undertaking in time and expense. If breeders offer many different dog breeds or too many litters of one breed, it is often a sign that all they care about is the sale. One more shortcoming: the more breeds that breeders offer, the lower the likelihood that they really have the requisite technical knowledge about the animals.

First Contact Point: the AKC

As a (potential) puppy purchaser you are always well advised to consult the American Kennel Club (AKC) or to visit an AKC dog show. There are also many aficionados of the breed present at national and international shows, in addition to registered breeders. (Show dates are available on

Good breeders have a waiting list of all the people who would like to get puppies from their kennel.

As soon as you make up your mind, add your name to the list to protect your selected puppy from other potential buyers.

Questions for the Future Dog Owner

No proper breeder sells his Frenchies over the phone or haggles over price, installment payments, or similar issues. In addition to the ample information he or she provides about his or her dogs, he or she is very likely to ask you a lot of questions, too. Ultimately, he or she wants to find the best, most appropriate, and most loving place for carefully raised puppies. At the instant when he or she entrusts you with a puppy, he or she hopes it will stay with you as long as it lives. He or she is counting on the fact that you are not buying the dog on a sudden whim, but rather that you are going to take care of it lovingly for many years.

Even if you are not used to answering so many questions, deal factually and honestly with the breeder; after all, his or her intention is not to stick his or her nose into your business, but rather to get an idea of how and where his or her puppy is going to live in the future.

He or she may ask about the following:
- whether you can demonstrate knowledge of the breed
- just why you have fallen in love with a French Bulldog
- what your lifestyle is like
- what your living situation is like and whether the landlord or the rules of the house allow dog ownership; in certain circumstances he or she may also want to see an appropriate letter of confirmation

- whether you have enough time for the dog
- how many hours a day your dog will have to spend alone at home if you are away at work
- if all family members are in agreement about getting a French Bulldog
- whether a family member has allergies (for example, to animal hair)
- whether you can pay for upkeep in the long run: veterinary costs, insurance, and food can be very costly
- whether you have a fenced yard and air conditioning
- whether you can take the dog along when you travel, or if it will be well cared for when you are gone
- whether you have the time, desire, and endurance to take care of the new family member for as long as a dog lives

How Much Does a French Bulldog Cost?

A proper breeder may charge up to two thousand dollars. This has nothing to do with the color you choose. Don't get taken in if someone tells you that the price is high because the animal has a very rare color. In that case, it's better to look for a different breeder.

The price is also not subject to negotiation. A serious breeder has firm prices but allows installment payments or similar conditions. Ultimately, a healthy female will cost you an average of $1,500. There are costs for the

equipment for the breeding site and regular kennel inspection with all the accompanying examinations, regular visits to the veterinarian, and proper food—so costs add up quickly, even before a single puppy sees the light of day.

Puppies at Last

Once you finally locate the right breeder, you probably will hardly be able to wait for your puppy to be born. In the old days, we had to wait for a long time for the first blurry photos, but now modern technology often makes it possible to marvel at the new family member for the first time just a few hours after birth. And many breeders offer the possibility through the Internet of following the puppies' daily growth and weight gain.

You probably will find your personal favorite in these first photos. If the breeder doesn't want to keep this little fellow for himself, it's highly likely that you will get your ideal candidate.

The breeder usually allows no-touch visits during the puppy's first weeks of life to guard against contagious diseases. When the puppy is eating solid food at eight to nine weeks old, has been checked for worms, and has received its vaccinations and its prepurchase health examination, it is ready to go to its new home.

The Last Weeks at the Breeder's

Shortly before the puppies move into their new homes, at eight weeks of age the first shots are due. A microchip is installed at the same time. The veterinarian implants a digital microchip

Basic training begins as early as the first weeks of life. Sit is an easy exercise that the little Frenchy will learn quickly with the bribe of a little treat.

Frenchies are faithful family dogs that also get along well with children.

with a unique number in the left side of the throat. The number is registered in its owner's name, and if the puppy is lost, it may be traced by the number. Microchip registration is a requirement in many countries (but not in the United States)—and thus a necessity if you later want to travel with the dog. Ask the seller if he or she has already had the puppy registered in an international data bank or if you need to take care of that yourself.

In some European countries, FCI pedigrees require many steps and the answers to many questions, which are different from the American AKC pedigree information requirements. European breed wardens are often referred to in canine literature and are purported to be an important step toward healthier dogs, which produce healthier puppies. Those wardens are specially trained individuals who may act in concert with dog breeders and their breed clubs to reduce genetic health problems that exist in purebred dogs.

In America, dog-breed wardens are sometimes referred to in foreign-bred dogs, perhaps principally in the German Shepherd breed, but the AKC pedigree requirements of all breeds are simpler. (Incidentally, the United States does not have breed wardens; breeders themselves are responsible for maintaining the quality of the breed.)

At long last, your chosen puppy can move to his permanent home and lucky family for the rest of his life.

When a puppy has reached its adoption age, the American breeder fills out a form that requires the puppy's name, registration number, colors and markings, competition titles, and any related physical and health information.

That health information may include its AKC–DNA registration information and other features that identify the puppy. Its microchip number is recorded as well, and in males, the presence or absence of scrotal testicles may be recorded. In the Frenchy, health information might possibly include tail set, any deformities such as undershot jaw or overbite, and so forth.

A Puppy Is Born

As future dog owners, people are very interested in being able to care for their puppies from the first minute of their lives. But responsible transfer of care is in the experienced hands of the breeder. The time of birthing and raising the puppies is very strenuous for everyone involved, and requires a high degree of concentration and specialized knowledge. Here you will get a glimpse of this exciting life phase.

In the first nine weeks, the tiny newborns, which at first are scarcely larger than a hand, grow into comical puppies. With growing curiosity, they explore their immediate surroundings, learn to eat solid food, and, with a little luck, even become nearly housetrained, and then they suddenly move into their new homes.

Pregnancy in French Bulldogs

The little Frenchies come into the world after a gestation period of about 63 days. This does not always happen naturally; sometimes the support of a veterinarian is required.

A handful of dog: the large eyes still can't see very well, but fortunately the well-developed sense of smell shows the way to the mother's teats.

The time between mating and the birth of the puppies flies by, until the breeder prepares the litter basket in a quiet room around two weeks before the calculated date of birth. This is where the puppies will enter the world and spend the first weeks with their mother. Until that point the dam can check out the facility at her leisure and try it out—bedded down on absorbent padding and soft blankets.

Many preparations must be made and all possible items need to be brought together. A thermometer, rubber gloves, disinfectant, petroleum jelly, and many cloth and paper towels should be available. Canine whelping can take a smooth, regular course or delivery may be intermittent. If in doubt about the timing and duration, call your veterinarian or an emergency veterinary clinic.

The Days Before the Birth

During gestation, in the fifth or sixth week after mating, the female generally is examined with ultrasound to ascertain whether she is pregnant. Three or four days before the calculated birth date, the female is X-rayed. In a natural birth the breeder thus knows that all the puppies have come into the world.

About 10 days before the calculated birth date the breeder takes the dam's temperature every day at the same time; if it has dropped from her normal 101.5°F to 99°F (39°C to 37.5°C) or lower, watch her carefully, because in all probability she will begin labor within a few hours.

The dog ceases eating but may still drink. She pants, is restless, and stares into the blankets and cushions in the litter basket. She keeps seeking a new corner for resting, or walks aimlessly through the room. All these indications are normal and are part of the birthing process; now she should not be left alone. Do not attempt to accelerate parturition with drugs. A short walk under strict supervision may help, but if it doesn't, call your veterinarian.

Sometimes it takes several hours for all the little Frenchies to see the light of day.

The Birth of the Puppies

The contractions begin the dilation phase, which can last up to 12 hours. During this time the uterine orifice opens wider because the puppies are pushing against it. The expulsion phase begins as soon as a puppy enters the birth canal. The fetal envelope bursts, and the amniotic fluid now serves as a lubricant; it should be clear and should not smell foul. Never apply pressure to the dam's abdomen.

Puppies are usually born head and forelegs first, and usually take a very short time to be born. If any part of the puppy, including its tail, appears with no further advancement of appearance, call your veterinarian immediately.

The veterinarian should also be consulted if there is any foul-smelling, brownish-green amniotic fluid, more than three hours have gone by since the water broke and no puppies have been born, or the rest phase between puppies lasts more than three hours. In both cases there is a suspicion that a baby is stuck in the birth canal or some other complications have arisen.

How long the birthing takes depends mainly on the mother's constitution and the number of puppies, among other things. The breeder will render assistance to his dog during the entire time (for example, by cutting the puppies' umbilical cords). The mother will lick the placental sac to reach her puppy, and it is normal

The floppy ear is no beauty flaw. The characteristic bat ears stand up sooner on some puppies and later on others.

What's in store for me out there? The puppy is still dependent on care from its mother and the breeder. But soon it will take over the world with its curiosity.

for her to swallow some of the placenta. Her licking stimulates the puppy's breathing.

If the puppies have to be delivered by caesarean section, the veterinary assistants and the breeder provide the initial care: they clear the newborn puppy's breathing passages of amniotic fluid or mucus, rub them with a terry towel, and place them onto a soft cushion under an infrared lamp.

In the meantime, the veterinarian takes care of the mother. As soon as she comes to from the anesthesia, the puppies are set in with her so they can get their first sip of milk. The breeder may have to help the puppies with this even in the case of a natural birth.

The Puppies Have Arrived

Once the litter is set with sucking milk, the breeder can examine each puppy at leisure, inspect it for deformities (e.g., cleft palate, harelip, stunted limbs), and record the date of birth, weight, and color markings. Sometimes it's necessary to gently massage a few drops of milk from the dam's teat and direct a puppy to this source of food.

The puppies' weight is recorded every day; if a puppy loses weight, a veterinarian must be consulted to determine the cause for the weight, loss. A healthy puppy does not lose weight, except perhaps on day 1. To the contrary, every day it gains a little and feels firm and taut.

When you are little, every movement requires great effort. After all the exertion, the puppy sometimes needs to stretch out all its limbs contentedly.

As the puppies are raised, all the particular characteristics of each one should be noted in the record, along with such things as the date of the first worming or shot, the day on which the puppies open their eyes, and the moment when they first hold up an ear. No matter how mundane these things may seem, they should all be recorded in writing.

From the first minutes, the tiny puppies need the most diligent care—and for the first week many concerned breeders sleep on an air mattress or a lounge chair right beside the litter basket. Like all puppies, little Frenchies are totally immature and dependent when they are born. Their eyes and ears are sealed shut at

birth, and for the first two to three weeks thereafter. The mother must continually lick the puppies after they suckle to encourage elimination of urine and droppings.

In the first weeks of life the breeder places the little ones at their mother's teats every two hours to make sure that every puppy gets enough milk. First-time mothers must learn to lie still so that all the puppies can drink their fill. The breeder doesn't just keep an eye out so that the littlest puppy always gets the best milk supply; ultimately, each one has to grow and thrive to the best of its ability. The breeder also makes sure that the teats are sucked uniformly so that they don't become inflamed,

Many breeders place a small paper cuff around the puppy's external ear to make it stand up sooner. Totally taping up the ear or putting a little stiffener inside, as was commonly done in the past, is no longer done, because this can easily lead to inflammation.

As they suckle, the little puppies knead the mother's teats industriously and sometimes energetically with their little paws to stimulate milk flow. In the process, they really suck hard on the teats. Their fast-growing, sharp claws need to be clipped regularly so they don't hurt the mother when the puppies are suckling. When a puppy is really sucking and you pull it away, you can hear a bubbling sound.

and there is no dangerous plugging of the milk ducts. But the young puppies also attempt to find their mother's teats, swinging their little heads back and forth to find their way to the milk bar.

The First Nine Weeks

• In technical jargon the first two weeks of life are known as the neonatal or vegetative phase. All the puppies are still totally helpless and quite inactive. But they are growing—and mightily. In the first 14 days, they triple their birth weight (and sometimes even more).

• After around two weeks the sense organs finally start to work properly. The puppies open their eyes and ears for the first time. In the third week of life the puppies also become aware of their littermates. They now sleep noticeably less and crawl around diligently in the litter basket. Now it is time for the mother Frenchy to start raising her little ones. Toward the end of the third week of life, all the senses are completely developed. By now the puppies have begun to crawl directionally, to move toward one another, and to play, squeal, and show alarm at strange noises or movements. They recognize their dam when she approaches.

From now on, the puppies can eat their first ground beef, in portions the size of the breeder's fingertip. Once they develop a taste for this treat, they can soon begin to eat from a shallow bowl. Now there must always be a small bowl of fresh

water or mild chamomile-fennel tea in the litter basket.

• Starting in the fourth week, some breeders feed a little baby food, yogurt, or cottage cheese in addition to the mother's milk—usually mixed with cracker crumbs. Frenchy puppies love this type of treat. Little by little the young puppies are fed with commercially available puppy food.

• Between the fourth and fifth week of life the first baby teeth poke through the gums and the Frenchies' ears begin to stand up. This generally doesn't happen to both ears at the same time, but rather one at a time. The ears may hang down again for a while when a puppy is changing teeth, but they will soon stand up again on their own.

At this age, when the weather is nice and warm, the puppies can play briefly in the yard. Fresh air is good for young dogs. And, finally, the future owners can also visit their new family member. This is a wonderful time for everyone.

• At six to seven weeks old the pups are finally weaned from their mother's milk—in part because now the dam reacts irritably when a puppy wants to suckle. Because of puppies' sharp teeth, nursing does not always take place without discomfort on the mother's part.

A conscientious breeder now also begins housetraining. After feeding the puppies, he or she puts them in a certain place so that they can relieve themselves. After they have done

In appearance the puppies still look a lot like one another—almost like peas in a pod. But now every puppy has its own personality.

their business, the little ones are effusively praised and petted; then comes a little nap for digestion.

• At eight weeks, the first shots are due and the puppies are microchipped by the veterinarian. At this time, the veterinarian will inspect every puppy thoroughly—and he or she does so gently and lovingly so that the dogs experience no fear of veterinarian visits later on.

• The litter has been examined and vaccinated by your veterinarian between six and eight weeks of age and should be ready for adoption. If any have not gone to new homes by the time the second vaccination is due, they should be returned for their boosters.

My Story

In 1973 there was a knock on Barbara Pallasky's apartment door. A young man wanted to sell her a magazine subscription. At his feet sat what looked like a strange combination of dog, rabbit, and cat. Barbara Pallasky didn't recognize the breed, but she was immediately fascinated by the strange little animal, even though she didn't yet know that it would change her life forever.

French Bulldogs have accompanied Barbara Pallasky and her family and shared their life for more than 35 years. Every one of them has been loved wholeheartedly.

When that man stood at my door with his peculiar companion, we quickly began conversing—about dogs in general and French Bulldogs in particular. That was the first French Bulldog I had ever seen. When we said good-bye, I had not only a new magazine subscription, but also the address of a Frenchy breeder. But it would still take quite a while for this first encounter to turn into the start of a great and lasting love.

Many years later when my mother became seriously ill, she longed for a small dog that could distract her from gloomy thoughts, give her hope, and provide enjoyment. And it came back: the memory of the French Bulldog. After the breeder that "my" magazine salesman had mentioned showed himself to be relatively dubious, I contacted the IKFB. Right in our area there was a litter of Frenchies, and one dark brindle female had not been spoken for. So in 1975 Chanel von Senilla moved in with my mother. She turned into a healthy, uncomplicated, and powerful dog and made my mother's life much easier and pleasanter.

I started to get deeply involved with this breed, found out about birthing in dogs, purebred-dog clubs, umbrella organizations and breeding requirements, pedigrees, and lots more.

Admittedly, I thought everything would be much easier. But my curiosity and interest were aroused.

One of my acquaintances raised Irish Setters. At her place I experienced my first dog birth—very simple and problem-free. We merely watched and counted the puppies. In the firm belief that things couldn't be any different with Frenchies, I made an appointment with my veterinarian and together we planned my Frenchy's first litter. The litter was born in 1978, the birth went normally, and out of seven puppies five survived. It was wonderful to watch how the tiny pups developed into magnificent "teenagers." I also will never forget the sad day when the new owners came to pick up our little ones. But all in all the positive aspects stand out—and that's why my kennel has now been in existence for more than 30 years.

My dogs have given me lots—and they still do. That's why I feel responsible to this breed. For 30 years I have been working as a volunteer for the International Club for French Bulldogs, which steadfastly pursues the principal goal of keeping the breed healthy and improving it. We want healthy, typical French Bulldogs. My last Frenchy will be in my will.

Frenchies simply are a part of Barbara Pallasky's life—whether on all fours or in her arms.

BARBARA PALLASKY is the first president of the
International Club for French Bulldogs. Since 1978, she has
been breeding her "vom Edelfluss" Frenchies. In 2009, she
received the Baron von Gingins Memorial Medal, the highest
distinction of the German Dog Association (VDH). The
association thereby endorsed her work, in which she insists
that ideal type and health need not contradict each other.

The Start of a
Wonderful Friendship

After a long time of pleasant anticipation and patient waiting, things have progressed: your little puppy is old enough to be brought home. At home, you have found the best provisions for making it as pleasant as possible for your new friend to acclimate. You have bought bowls and toys from a pet shop and found the best spot in the house for the dog's bed. An exciting time is beginning—not just for you, but also for the new four-legged family member. Plan for enough free time in the next two to three weeks, for the little dog has a lot to learn, starting with the first training attempts and housetraining. It will need your help with this. Also, for the little Frenchy's inner life, it is absolutely necessary that the new family have plenty of time for it in the coming weeks. It's best to discuss with your family who will take over which tasks and who will be available for the puppy and when. Write down a little daily schedule that lists all the routine duties, such as feeding times and walks. A recurring routine makes it easier for the puppy to adjust to its new surroundings. Along with all the responsibility and adjustment, enjoy this time—puppyhood is a unique life phase for both you and your dog.

A Matter of Conscience: Male or Female

When a dog moves in, the question of male or female is a primary concern. With this breed, the sexes are not so different in disposition. Besides, usually the choice of a puppy at the breeder's is an affair of the heart: many times dog owners who positively wanted a male fall in love with a little female, and vice versa.

Males often are very patient. What drives a female up the wall may not bother males for a long time.

As with nearly all creatures, female Frenchies are smaller and more feminine than the males, whose maximum allowable weight, according to the standard, is 28 pounds (12.7 kg). Generally, males are bulkier and larger than females, who also should weigh significantly less.

You should consider in advance what your daily life with your dog will be like: if you live in an area with lots of male dogs, things can get quite complicated with a female in heat, and, at one time or another, your yard will have to withstand a siege by other animals.

An unneutered male in an area with lots of females, on the other hand, may make the rounds and run away. If you intend to turn your dog over to a boarding kennel or to a dog sitter on a regular basis, you need to be aware that unneutered males may not be always welcome, especially by a dog sitter.

Typical Female

It is continually claimed that female dogs are easier to train than males, that they learn more quickly, and are more gentle and affectionate. On the other hand, the female sex supposedly also tends toward moodiness and sometimes acts like a little diva.

In practice, it is not possible to confirm whether all this is usual bias. For all these characteristics, there are classic examples as well as counterexamples.

But one thing you need to consider in any case if you are contemplating a female: every six months she will go into heat. In this two- to three-week cycle the little lady turns into an irresistible attraction for all the males in the surrounding area. The routine walk can quickly turn into a gauntlet run. In the proestrus stage the female will still stave off every male. But from the tenth day on she will be receptive whenever a male approaches. If you are not alert, things will go to the extreme. If you don't want to raise puppies, spaying is sure protection against unwanted pregnancy.

What About a Male?

In contrast to many other breeds, male French Bulldogs do not act really dominant or combative. As a result, they rarely get involved in fights. Still, a male Frenchy is a real he-man: he is alert, curious, and always eager to defend his territory. And, yet for all that, he is no rambunctious barker, and normally is also affectionate and not very moody. Thus, the lovable cuddler is generally just as easy to train as a female. From time to time a little more self-assertiveness on your part simply may be required, for male Frenchies are a little obstinate.

Neutering

With females, spaying can be advantageous for various medical reasons. For example, spaying

Consult your veterinarian for alternatives to neutering and do not buy over-the-counter products to prevent pregnancy in your female or others that purportedly cool off an ardent male. Some chemicals are dangerous, and others are rarely successful.

reduces the risk of mammary tumors, tumors in the milk glands, and uterine suppuration. But since French Bulldogs are among those dogs that are late developers, the surgery should not be done too early. Consult your veterinarian; he or she will examine your Frenchy and can tell you when the surgery is safest.

Some breeders believe that early spaying will retard growth or change personality in Frenchies, but others disagree, and many have found that the danger of mis-mating offsets the possibility of retardation or attitude changes. All in all, neutering early keeps the dog more puppylike and increases urinary incontinence. What at first may sound cute is not always a desirable condition for the dog. Only a completely developed animal has the necessary behavior repertory to deal with its environment.

What applies to the female applies all the more to the male: it is not fully grown until the age of two and a half and thus should not be neutered before the second year of life, if at all. The operation makes sense if there are sexually mature female dogs in the family (in this case, it is usually better to spay the female). Also, if the dog has an exaggerated sexual drive, you should consider having it neutered.

The Basic Equipment

Once the puppy moves in, he or she requires your complete attention. To prevent unnecessary stress, you should get all the necessary things in advance that your new resident will need from day one.

A nice, soft cushy bed like this one is every Frenchy's dream.

Collar and Leash

A nylon collar about ¼ inch (0.5 cm) wide and adjustable for length, which can grow along with the dog in the coming weeks and months, is appropriate for your puppy. The collar should always be adjusted so that it does not constrict the sensitive throat, yet does not allow the puppy to slip out of it. The collar is adjusted properly when you can comfortably fit one finger between the dog's throat and the collar.

Leather collars should have no harsh stitching or rivets on the underside. Choose a type that is as soft as possible, preferably padded, and not too wide. The Bulldog's hairs break easily, leaving unattractive marks in the coat. Here, too, the collar must not be too tight, and in due time it must be replaced with a larger one, using the finger test.

A harness is not recommended for puppies, because generally it takes them much longer to learn to walk properly on the leash. But if your dog has problems with his or her neck vertebrae, a harness may take some pressure off these parts.

A 3-foot (1 m) adjustable nylon or leather leash that works with the collar is also recommended. Retractable leashes are not for young Bulldogs: they merely lure the youngsters into developing their own running style. They scoot back and forth, hither and yon, and every which way, instead of simply straight ahead. The light pull required to draw a retractable leash out of its handle also quickly teaches the dog from an early age to pull on the leash.

Sleeping Area

French Bulldogs love soft, plush beds. But many of these models require washing by hand and thus require lots of care. When you buy a bed, make sure it can be washed at 104°F (40°C) and dried. One tip: if you put a tennis ball into the dryer, the plush fabric remains fuzzy.

Under no circumstances should you get a wicker bed. It will tempt the little puppy to gnaw excessively—and at some point when he or she is out of sight for a moment, he or she will also

Ceramic bowls are easy to wash and look good for a long time. Another plus: they keep drinking water nice and cool in the summer.

There are many attractive containers for storing treats. Make sure they are easy to clean and can be closed tightly so that no pests can take up residence.

tamper with your furniture. Aside from that, the puppy could swallow a piece of wicker; in the worst case, the sharp splinters could get stuck in the short, narrow, fleshy throat. That can be life threatening.

The ideal place for a dog bed is a quiet corner where there is no draft and from which the Frenchy can see everything. Right from the beginning you should consider whether or not you want your dog in the bedroom with you at night.

Food and Water Dishes

Stainless-steel bowls are easy to clean and can even be put into the dishwasher. In the summer, clay or ceramic bowls are appropriate, because the water in them stays cool longer. Another advantage of these materials is that the bowls are relatively heavy and therefore more stable—even when your Frenchy is particularly hungry and eats greedily. Plastic bowls, on the other hand, easily slide around and tempt the dog to gnaw on them.

The bowl should be large enough to hold the portion of food, and to keep the Frenchy from spreading half of it over the floor while eating. The water bowl should also provide enough room for your dog to drink comfortably.

Food

Your breeder will already have told you what he feeds his puppies. Always buy a medium-size

bag of this food so that the little tummy doesn't experience any problems right on the first day. In most cases the breeder will give you some of the appropriate food.

Toys

A French Bulldog can keep busy with its toys for hours—and not just during puppyhood. A ball or two or some rubber squeak toys should therefore always be available. Your dog can have a great time with these. For playing together with your dog, natural rubber balls on ropes, pull ropes, and even Frisbees have proven their worth. French Bulldogs are more athletic than they may appear at first glance.

But stones and wood (even little sticks) are not appropriate toys. The former are bad for the teeth, and with the latter, as with wicker beds, there is a danger of injury and choking. Old shoes and articles of clothing should also be taboo, since your dog can't distinguish between old and new—and thus soon will also chew on clothing that you still want to wear.

Travel Crate

Transporting the dog in a secure travel crate starts as early as the trip home from the breeder's. You will use this later on, too, when you need to transport your Frenchy. A travel crate can also serve well in the home, for example, when your dog is not yet housetrained and doesn't need to be wandering all over the house.

1. & 4. Balls on ropes, a knotted rope, and a rubber squeak toy, plus a knotted dish towel, are great pastimes and usually will be enthusiastically received as toys.

2. A soft leather collar nicely decorated with small stones or embroidery, plus an appropriate leash, dress up the Frenchy. The collar should not be too wide; rivets and eyelets should be backed with leather to avoid breaking the hairs.

3. Giving your Frenchy a rubdown with a massage glove amounts to a wellness treatment. You not only rub away loose hairs and particles of dirt, but also stimulate circulation. No wonder so many dogs react to it with a real orgy of grunting.

French Bulldogs' coat care is kept to a minimum because of the short hair. A soft, natural-bristle hairbrush or a glove with little rubber knobs is fine for coat care. Dandruff is best removed with a microfiber dustcloth or a regular soft towel.

When you travel by car, place the crate securely in the backseat—preferably in combination with a dog crate. The dog should be properly secured in the car. The dog and occupanats can be severely injured in an accident if the dog flies through the passenger compartment upon impact. In addition, many accidents are caused by unsecured dogs in a vehicle. When you buy a travel crate, pay attention to the quality (especially the closure and the grating) and to the size. Your dog should be able to stand comfortably and turn around inside, but not have too much room for rambunctious gymnastics. Get advice from a pet shop.

An alternative for car travel is a special harness that is secured to the rear seat and fastened to the seat-belt system.

(© Shutterstock)

1

2

3

4

A collar and a leash are essential for walking the Frenchy safely. A harness is recommended only when your dog is older or has problems with its vertebrae. A harness often keeps puppies from learning how to walk properly on a leash.

Solid ceramic or stainless-steel dishes can even become eye-catchers in the home, as you can see here.

A cozy dog bed is a requirement. But avoid too much fur and plush fabric, because a Frenchy will chew on it, and the fibers could get stuck in its throat.

You can never have too many soft blankets and towels. That way you are well equipped if your Frenchy gets wet or you want to set up a temporary bed.

The First Days in the New Home

Home at last! Everything is still new and unfamiliar to the puppy. But with your help, he or she will soon feel as secure as he or she did with her mother and siblings. Then he or she will know: "This is my place."

Saying good-bye to the foster parents, mom, and the siblings. Often the breeder is more distressed than the puppy when it's time to move to the new home.

To soften the blow of parting, a couple of weeks in advance you should leave a blanket at the breeder's; later, during the trip home, it will smell like the puppy's mother and siblings.

The Way Home

Once all the formalities, especially the purchase contract and payment, are taken care of, it's time to head home with your Frenchy. If you have to travel by car, you should have at least one other companion. Especially for longer trips, it can become stressful if you are traveling alone with the puppy.

Generally, the puppy is quite disoriented and worried during its first trip. Everything is new and different, and it feels lonely and begins to whine and whimper. No wonder: he or she has just had to leave familiar surroundings, mother, and siblings. That's why he or she needs your comforting. It's best if you sit next to the securely restrained puppy on the backseat and give it lots of attention during the trip. That will calm the little one down and help you bond, for your dog will learn that you are an attentive companion who will stand by him or her even in an emergency.

Always keep a package of moist wipes handy just in case the puppy feels carsick and throws up. On fairly long trips, take a break so that the puppy can do its business. But in no case let him or her run free. The puppy does not know you and will not obey you; in the worst case, he or she may even run away.

Welcome Home

Once you arrive home, the first thing is to go outdoors. After the exciting drive, the little animal surely will have to do its business and wants to explore the new surroundings. Give your new resident enough time to take care of this.

After a few minutes, you can show the new arrival its new home. Again let him or her sniff and look around thoroughly. Show the dog its water bowl, which from now on will always be in the same place and available at all times.

Show the puppy the new sleeping spot. The puppy will thus learn quickly that this is its safe haven. And, since your little Frenchy still needs lots of sleep, you should give it this time whenever it is tired.

Once the initial excitement subsides, give the puppy a little between-meals treat at the feeding place (e.g., a little hamburger). After the puppy eats, immediately take it outdoors so that it can do its business (it surely knows this procedure from the breeder). When it does its business properly, praise and pet the puppy abundantly and then bring it back indoors.

Perhaps one of the most important rules for the beginning: in the first days, avoid inviting lots of friends and acquaintances to gaze in admiration at your puppy. They all will have plenty of time to deal with the Frenchy in the coming years. For now the puppy has enough new impressions to process. And he or she first needs to get used to you, right?

The First Night in the New Home

During the day, the new home should be stimulating and interesting. But no later than the first night, your little Frenchy will miss her mother and siblings and will feel terribly lonely. You can soothe the pain of separation if you put another dog bed right next to yours. That way you can comfortably pet the puppy from your bed. That way she will feel secure and soon build up trust in you. Another advantage: you will immediately notice if the puppy becomes restless and needs to go out.

Don't be weak and take the poor, helpless creature into your bed. Otherwise he or she will always want to be with you. The young dog

Generally, the breeder will give you a familiar toy to take on the trip home, in addition to a little basic equipment such as puppy food and body-building compounds. That way, the little dog finds some familiar objects in the new home and feels the separation less acutely.

*A move involves so much
excitement. The many
impressions are very taxing
for the puppy, and he or she
soon sleeps in exhaustion in
his or her new master's arms.
But the people also have to
get used to the little boarder.*

must learn right from the first that the master
and mistress's bed is off-limits.

If you don't want the dog to sleep in your
bedroom in the long run, it's a good idea to
avoid that right from the start. In order to
spend the first night near the dog, place its bed
near the sofa or make yourself comfortable on
an air mattress. Close your door or put a baby
gate in the doorway if you don't want the dog to
take a night stroll into your room. That way he
or she can see you, but not get into the room.

Housetraining

In the first days and weeks, don't scold the dog
if you occasionally find a little puddle or pile on
the floor. At this age, your puppy simply is not
housetrained. With time, he or she will learn to
control elimination.

Bring your Frenchy outdoors first thing in
the morning after you get up, after every meal,
and in the evening before you go to bed. And
whenever the puppy starts sniffing intently and
becomes restless, it should get outdoors as
quickly as possible. As soon as it gets into the
elimination stance, immediately pick it up with
an energetic "Yuck!" or "No!" and carry it out
to the yard to do its business.

Did a little puddle appear on the floor when
you were not paying attention? In this case, it is
totally useless to scold the dog when you discover the misdeed. The dog simply cannot
understand why you are so angry with it.

Only when you catch the dog red-handed can you reprimand him or her with a loud "Yuck!" or a clap of the hands. And, even if it's already too late, immediately put the dog outside so it can finish the process. Then praise it effusively and maybe even give it a little treat.

Practicing Being Alone

Obviously, a dog—especially a puppy—should not often be left alone. But, of course, sometimes that cannot be avoided, and the dog will have to spend a couple of hours in the house or the apartment without you. Therefore, it is important to practice being alone as early as possible. It is very easy: leave the room, close the door behind you, and wait a few minutes before you "come back home." Praise the dog effusively if it was well behaved, and give it a treat.

Very important: do not weaken if the dog whimpers and howls while you are out of the room. If you do, the only thing the dog will learn is that you come back when it "calls"

you—and it will continue to do this. But if you remain steadfast, the dog quickly understands that whining leads nowhere, and in the future it will refrain from doing so.

If you come back to find that your Frenchy is on a rampage, you can scold him or her in a severe tone of voice. But the situation is different if he or she has already caused damage and runs up to you joyfully; then, unfortunately, it is too late for scolding. The dog would connect your displeasure with her greeting and would justifiably become insecure. Simply ignore the dog; that is adequate "punishment."

After a few days stay away a little longer (e.g., take the trash out). Later on, run a couple of quick errands or go around the block, until your dog manages to spend a couple of hours alone without getting into any nonsense. Even if the puppy keeps chewing some things, it's better not to put everything away or out of its reach. Otherwise, your Frenchy will never learn how he or she is supposed to behave. Remain consistent and persevere in your practice.

This bed is awesome;
I'll just stay right here.

Small children and French Bulldogs: nothing attracts more attention than a team like this one. Usually, children pick up their love for Frenchies in the cradle, since mom, dad, grandma, and grandpa have been infected with Frenchy fever for years—and this enthusiasm is highly contagious.

This breed is characterized by its gentle, patient disposition with children. What child would not be proud to have such playmates?

83

FREE TIME
WITH A FRENCHY

French Bulldogs are real family dogs. They love nothing better than always being with their humans, playing with them, cuddling, and accompanying them wherever they go. But a few rules still apply.

Occupation and Training

Dogs need systematic training right from the start, particularly the lovable and headstrong French Bulldog. These dogs have their own minds and require lots of patience and persistence on your part. But it's worth the trouble: ultimately, there is nothing more trying than a disobedient dog that tugs on the leash and gnaws on furniture and shoes at home.

   With firm rules and daily practice, your Frenchy will learn to accept you as the leader of the pack. If you are inconsistent and let it get away with things, it will soon want to take over the leading role in the human-dog pack and will challenge your commands in the future. Nothing but joint practice strengthens the human-dog team; and you can even use playtime to strengthen your bond. Your French Bulldog can have a good romp while practicing basic commands, such as Come!

Training Required

For sure, a French Bulldog is no Labrador Retriever that learns quickly and always wants to perform new tasks. This breed has its own mind. Still, your Frenchy should know the basic training rules and obey them on command. That's the only way you will be able to take her everywhere without problems.

Every Frenchy can learn how to sit—and should keep practicing this command over and over so that it doesn't forget.

Right from the start, it's a good idea to practice the command *lie down* at the end of a walk. Your Frenchy is already a little tired and will lie down more willingly than when it has just begun to romp.

Walking on a Leash

One of the first things your puppy should learn is how to walk properly on a leash. To practice this, first put the collar onto the Frenchy (you should always be able to fit one finger comfortably between her neck and the collar).

Give the dog time to get used to the collar. If you play with the dog a lot, it will quickly accept the collar as the most natural thing in the world.

Once this is accomplished, clip on the leash and go for a walk. Give the command, "Heel!" Try to walk in front of your dog, and draw its attention to you so that it follows you briskly. Sometimes a toy that interests the dog helps. Still, it may take a while before the Frenchy trots along. Keep trying, and in no case pull the dog along behind you impatiently.

Make sure that the leash always remains nice and loose. The dog must not pull. If it does, stay in one spot and ignore it until it turns toward you. Now praise the dog and walk on. If the dog follows on a loose leash, praise him or her some more. If you give the command *heel* at the same time, the dog will quickly learn what it is to do upon hearing the command.

Sit

For your dog to learn to sit on command, all it takes is a little patience and a quantity of treats. Hold one over its head so that it has to sit to see the treat better. Say the command *"Sit"* as soon as the dog sits properly; give it the treat while you simultaneously praise and pet the dog.

Lie Down

If your Frenchy can master the command *sit*, it can learn to lie down. Have the dog sit, and then move the treat slowly to the floor and then to the front. That way, your sweet-toothed dog will automatically lie down. Say the command *"Lie down"* as soon as the dog lies down properly; give it the treat, and praise it generously. Once the dog eats the treat, have him or her sit once more and end the exercise.

Come

When you call your Frenchy, it should come to you as quickly as possible—for its own safety, for example, in street traffic. At the outset, you can practice this quite playfully. When you have the dog's food ready, call it with a friendly *"Come!"* and praise it generously when it runs joyfully to you. Then it gets the food.

Once the dog understands that there is something to eat after the command, call it several times a day in the house. If it comes quickly rather than plodding along, there is a treat waiting in addition to the mandatory praise.

As soon as the dog comes to you reliably in the house, you can move the training outdoors. Here, there are many more interesting things to distract the puppy, so it's a good idea to keep it on a long, thin (retractable) leash so you can reel it in quickly in an emergency.

You should not spare the praise, petting, and treats as you teach your Frenchy to come to you willingly.

Never scold, even if the dog is slow to react at first. That would teach the dog that it will be punished when it goes to you—and the next time it would dawdle even longer.

Frenchies need consistent training, such as companion dog instruction. Then, they lie calmly in the grass and patiently and attentively wait for the next command.

Well-trained, socialized Frenchies play good-naturedly, even in a pack, without brawling. Here, four dogs from different families are having fun meeting, and in spite of the great heat there are no quarrels.

Begging

No doubt about it: a French Bulldog is a perfect master at wide-eyed begging for food at the table or in the kitchen.

"I am so hungry, poor, and unloved"—it is very difficult to resist this particular gaze. But remain steadfast, for once it works, your dog will keep trying it, which can become quite annoying in the long run.

In addition, Frenchies salivate and slobber with lots of foods. They also gain weight faster than other breeds.

From the outset a firm, consistent *no* at the table may indeed take a little willpower. But it will save lots of annoyance, and it will benefit your dog's health.

Jumping Up

French Bulldogs have a tendency to jump up on people—perhaps to greet them or perhaps to invite more petting. That may appear comical, but dirty paw prints, runs in stockings, and scratches on bare legs are disagreeable.

To keep your Frenchy from developing the habit of greeting you so impetuously, ignore it every time it jumps. Pet it only when all four paws are on the floor. Also instruct your visitors to do the same.

If you are consistent, the Frenchy will very soon learn that restrained behavior produces quicker and more abundant petting.

With respect to praise: a treat should be an extra that the dog finds worth exerting itself for.

This works only if you refrain from continually slipping it something to munch without cause. Give your Frenchy a treat only when she has complied thoroughly with your wishes.

In Dog School

Even if you practice regularly at home, a visit to a puppy school is always advisable. There, the puppy can play with other dogs of a similar age and learn proper social behavior. And knowing how it must behave with other dogs will keep your daily walks from turning into a gauntlet run.

Puppy schools also often have play equipment that can be found only at dog-training facilities: tunnels in which the little dogs can hide, big boxes with lots of colorful balls, a slide—these are the greatest entertainment for your puppy. You will also pick up some valuable tips for training and care.

Many clubs and private dog trainers offer advanced courses and companion dog training after your dog has completed puppy school; check the Internet or the newspaper for opportunities for advanced courses or companion training in your area

Left: Frenchies are eager learners. With a handful of treats you can get them to do the neatest tricks, such as "give me a high-five."

Right: Never practice longer than 10 to 15 minutes at a time; otherwise, the Frenchy will lose interest. It is also important to end training with a success. If things aren't working, have the dog do something simpler. Praise it and end the training session. Try the newer command again the next time.

Frenchies and Other Dogs

In general, French Bulldogs are peaceful dogs —yet there still can be occasional problems with other dogs. This almost always is because of the Frenchy's special facial expressions and physique, which significantly limit its body language.

The Frenchy's faults seem to present no problems in living with humans. On the contrary, French Bulldogs have almost human facial expressions, and can use them to "converse" and communicate perfectly with their owners. Many also emit soft sounds—for example when they want a treat or some petting—and they are really irresistible.

In contrast to us humans, dogs do not communicate with words. Instead, they bark and growl—but they especially "speak" with their bodies. For example, their posture and the placement of their tails communicate from a distance just how they feel: they make themselves large to create the most domineering effect, and small when they are afraid. They wag their tails energetically when they are excited and turn their heads to the side when they want to avoid trouble.

At shorter distances, dogs use the position of their ears and their facial expressions to communicate with one another. For example, they narrow their eyes, curl their chops, or pull their ears back, thereby sending unmistakable signals to their surroundings.

When you look at a French Bulldog, you see at first glance that simply in terms of physique it is different from other breeds. In some instances, this leads to misunderstandings or annoyances in communication with other dogs.

The Frenchy's Body Language

Because of its appearance, a French Bulldog cannot always express itself intelligibly. A German Shepherd, for example, can approach other dogs while wagging its tail, hold its tail up in a macho way, or tuck it between its hind legs—but the nearly tailless Frenchy is nearly "speechless" in this regard. At most, it can wag its stubby tail a little bit and almost unnoticeably. Even experienced Frenchy owners often have difficulties perceiving and interpreting this signal properly, so it's no wonder that from time to time there are misunderstandings with other dogs (and humans).

This problem is not helped by the fact that the Frenchy has a tendency toward hubris and delusions of grandeur. Try to steer this characteristic in the right direction from the very beginning by observing it very closely in play, so you can avoid difficulties later on when you go for a walk.

Because of their short snouts, French Bulldogs breathe more loudly than most other breeds, and this also leads to misunderstandings. Other dogs often interpret the loud breathing as growling—and depending on their disposition, they can react to it with unwarranted anxiety or aggression.

Attentive Observer

With a little practice you can read a French Bulldog's current mood: if its posture is erect, the ears are upright, and the chops are relaxed, the Frenchy is relaxed. But this doesn't mean that it is not watching its immediate surroundings attentively so it doesn't miss anything. If anything piques its interest, it stretches out its neck, turns its ears slightly, and tenses its muscles. Worry lines also form on its face.

The countless wrinkles that make the French Bulldog's face so unmistakable and lovable also significantly restrict its facial expressions in communicating with other dogs.

Display Behavior

If a Frenchy, whether male or female, wants to let another dog know how big and powerful it is, it prances with its head held high and steps lively on its cat paws.

Despite its massive body it looks like a little elf. If this doesn't produce the desired effect, the dog ramps up the display behavior to a threat. Now a soft, muffled growl can be heard, the chops curl upward almost imperceptibly, the eyes take on a fixed gaze, and the hairs along the spine (ridge) stand up. A little volcano is about to erupt.

Usually, this is enough to put the other dog in its place, for in the face of this type of threat, many opponents quickly take to their heels.

In only the rarest cases, will a Frenchy show truly aggressive behavior. At the bottom of its heart, it is ultimately a good-natured, comical, and lovable dog that would like nothing better than to play and cuddle all day.

Submissiveness

Like all dogs, the Frenchy displays submissive behavior by lying on its back and putting its paws against the chest or the head of its opponent. Slight smacking noises that result from licking its own nose are also a sign that your dog is knuckling under.

Playing

French Bulldogs remain playful into a ripe old age. They get the greatest pleasure from chewing on rubber squeak toys and chasing balls and frisbees, and they love a tug-of-war. But you are still the best playmate for them.

When you play, make sure that the floor is not too slippery (as with, for example, parquet flooring and tiles). On a slippery surface, your Frenchy can easily experience a muscle strain or injure itself in other ways.

Playing is always important for your pet's development and well-being. But it's just as important that the dog observe a few rules in the process. Otherwise a playful tussle over a rope, for example, can quickly turn into a bona-fide power struggle.

Since Frenchies generally are a bit obstinate, you will sometimes need a clear rebuke. If you are firm and consistent in forbidding bad behavior, your dog will eventually understand what is permitted and what is not.

You Determine the Playtimes

Even in matters of pleasure your dog needs to know who is the master (or the mistress) of the house. If the dog invites you to play, you can calmly ignore it.

The fun begins only when you take the initiative. Of course, it may sometimes happen that your Frenchy doesn't feel like playing at that moment. Don't force the issue, for both parties need to have fun together.

What applies to the invitation to play is also valid for finishing up: it's not the dog that decides when the play is over, but rather you. Make sure to end before your dog loses interest in the game. That way you remain an interesting playmate—and the next time your Frenchy will again pitch in willingly.

Learning the Pecking Order in a Playful Way

Don't let your dog get away with anything during playtime that you normally forbid (for example, jumping up on its hind legs). That is an irritation to the dog, because it cannot distinguish between the situations. Also, make sure that the pecking order remains intact during play. For example, don't always let the dog win in a tug-of-war, don't run away to make the dog chase you, and don't let the dog get the upper hand. This is especially important when a child plays with the dog.

No Biting

A Frenchy puppy has very sharp teeth. When the dog nips, it can really hurt, even though the dog doesn't have the power of a full-grown French Bulldog. Make it clear from the outset that you don't tolerate any snapping. If the dog becomes too rambunctious during play, immediately pull your hand back, stop the game, and show the dog unmistakably that this behavior is forbidden (usually a harsh "Yuck!" is all it takes). Then ignore the dog and let it amuse itself for a while. Let some time go by before the next invitation to play together. Generally, dogs learn quickly that they need to obey—even if sometimes they still get a little rowdy.

Frenchies and Children

Their moderate size, their even-tempered, intrepid disposition, and their amazing patience mean that French Bulldogs are great dogs for children. Cuddling on the sofa, going for a walk, and playing in the yard are great fun for both playmates.

Once a child learns what a dog needs, the friendship can last a lifetime.

French Bulldogs are real family dogs, so they are tireless playmates when there are children in the house—and the youngster will receive their unlimited attention. But a small dog like this is not only suited to play: it also has a teaching benefit and truly therapeutic capabilities.

On the one hand, children learn that they must assume responsibility for the four-legged companion: the dog must be fed every day and go for a walk, and it wants to be groomed, challenged, and, of course, petted. Even the smallest children can help with this by performing such duties as filling the water bowl, helping to get the food ready, or putting the collar on the dog

under parental supervision. All this encourages a child's social competence.

But many times the dog is not only a four-legged fellow resident for the youngest family members, but also a best friend. The dog will never make fun of them, and will never betray them or insult them. In addition, the youngster will spend a significant amount of time exercising in the fresh air, which has a positive effect on health and overall development.

For a Good Life Together

To keep the relationship between child and dog as intact as possible, everyone must observe certain rules. The Frenchy must accept that it is lower than the people in the pecking order, even if one of the humans is much smaller than the master or mistress. The dog must learn from the outset not to harass the child physically, even if the child is not as strong as the dog. The dog must not jump up on the child: the puppy may still be tiny, but a full-grown Frenchy can easily knock a child over.

Also, if the puppy bites a hand too hard in play with its needle-sharp teeth, interrupt the play immediately and give the dog a harsh command ("Yuck!"). Usually, this reaction is sufficiently intimidating for the puppy—and even more so if the child also yells loudly or cries.

Forbid games in which the child and the dog pull on anything (such as a rope or toy), too.

A team step by step. Still, child and dog must observe some rules during play.

The Frenchy will quickly notice that it is winning—and take itself too seriously.

Children too need to observe certain rules: they must learn that their four-legged friend is not a toy and that there are times when it wants to be left alone—for example, when it eats, drinks, or lies down in bed. There are a few behavior recommendations that apply to all dogs. Children should:

- never pull on the bat ears or the little tail—even though this may be highly tempting to very little children.
- never stare directly into a Frenchy's eyes. In dog language, this is a sign that two antagonists are measuring each other up.
- not try to take a toy or a treat away from the dog. The dog may defend ownership and snap.
- never run away from a Frenchy, even when they are afraid or want to play. The dog probably will give chase—and it is faster and stronger.
- never get into the middle if the Frenchy gets into a fight with another dog. In the excitement of the fight, one of the dogs might bite the child.

My Story

Only through skillful persuasion did Angelika Meier, the owner of the charming Jeanny von der Rothenberg Festung, succeed in purchasing the very promising female dog from the breeder Susanne Saller-Schneider. Gina was really supposed to remain at the breeder's home. But, in December 2009, Gina, as the pinto Frenchy was then named, moved in with Mrs. Meier and her two French Bulldogs, Abby and Finesse.

Who is prouder? The docile Gina or her owner, Angelika Meier? She showed the other tracking dog owners that size is not everything.

None of my Frenchies are spoiled watchdogs. They are "proper" dogs, but of course that does not mean that they don't sometimes like to lie around on the couch. But I give them plenty to do every day, such as dog sports. That way they are more even-tempered and don't get into so much nonsense at home.

When Gina showed that she liked to sniff around on the ground and turn up the most diverse things, I thought, "Why shouldn't we try her out on tracking?" The first time we found ourselves on the training field among Boxers, German Shepherds, mixed breeds, and Giant Schnauzers. Of course at first people smiled at us sympathetically. Who ever heard of a French Bulldog working as a tracker? Terriers and Dachshunds, sure, you see that fairly often, for these breeds are also trained for the hunt. But a companion dog? We didn't let ourselves get discouraged, and soon the humorous remarks stopped. Soon my little Frenchy was following the trails faster than many larger dogs.

The first segment went straight ahead for about 50 feet (15 m). I placed a piece of hot dog in every footprint. I took Gina on the lead, pointed, and gave the energetic command, "Search!" The Frenchy didn't need to be told twice. She immediately started the search, ferreted out piece after piece of hot dog, and found a whole handful of them at the end, to her great delight.

We practiced this way twice a week for about a month. Then we added the first turn. Here too Gina performed her duty admirably. And if she ever lost the scent, I didn't scold her, but simply waited patiently until she picked it up again by herself.

Four weeks later I increased the difficulty again: Gina had to locate a sock that I had "lost." At the same time I cut back on the treats—surely to the disappointment of my greedy little dog. When she nevertheless searched and stood before the sock to show that she had found it, of course she got an appropriate reward. With time the trails became longer and more difficult. Now I hardly use any treats. The leash is more than 30 feet (10 m) long, and Gina keeps on moving straight ahead, as she should while tracking.

My next goal: I would like to take some tracking tests with Gina. I practice with Gina every day and hide little treats at home for her to search out. I'm sure that she will pass the test, for Gina has a really good nose for tracking.

How it should work: the nose seems to stick to the ground when the dog is searching for the right trail.

ANGELIKA MEIER, a Boxer and Frenchy breeder, had a boarding kennel for many years and worked as a dog trainer. Gina is not only an outstanding tracker, but has also participated in and placed high in various international shows, and has easily passed the breeding suitability test. Angelika Meier is now looking forward to the first litter of puppies.

Frenchy Shows

Even if they don't intend to raise puppies themselves, many Frenchy owners show their dogs. If you also entertain this idea, you should address it when you buy your Frenchy, because not every dog is appropriate for the show ring. Even if it is very handsome, a nervous or shy Frenchy will never show its entire typical beauty in a strange environment. A dog show also involves a huge amount of stress for the dog; the presence of many other dogs and the usual greater number of strange people are unsettling. This does not do either you or the dog any favors.

If you are looking for a show dog, you should select a puppy with a fundamentally stable, even disposition. Your breeder can advise you on this: he or she knows whether a puppy is more reserved or self-assured, curious, and adventurous, and thus will step into the ring with more confidence and pride.

In the Ring with the Dog

Even in puppyhood it is possible to evaluate a dog's character. Select the appropriate dog, for dog shows should be enjoyable not only for you, but also for the dog.

If you belong to a dog association, you may have the opportunity to receive a monthly magazine. Or you can get it online. Such magazines often contain a calendar of dog shows. Once you settle on a location and date, a registration for your dog is also required. This is usually paid in advance.

Alternatively, you may be able to sign your dog up for a show online. The costs will be specified in the relevant promotional information. Smaller shows organized by French Bulldog associations independently of the national clubs will involve a registration fee, too.

If you miss the payment deadline, you may be able to take care of it on-site. Otherwise, your dog may not be allowed to take part in the show. In any case, find out the customary procedure in advance. Travel and preparation take some time, and it would be a shame if you were not allowed in.

Getting Ready

Once you have decided to participate in a show with your dog, get in touch with your breeder. Nothing makes him or her feel more honored than when animals from the kennel are shown to a broad public (unless he or she sold it as a non-show-quality dog). The kennel owner will thus help you with your plans, for if you want to show your dog successfully, there are a few things to keep in mind.

• You certainly have noticed in visiting a dog show that the important thing is not just the dog's appearance, but also its behavior in the ring.

For example, a show dog must remain totally unruffled when an unknown judge touches its ears or wants to inspect individual limbs. Practice this in advance with your dog. Ask friends to help you with this. This is good training for the ring.

First, lift the dog onto a table and speak reassuringly to it so that it remains still. In the next training step, try to place its legs parallel to each other (no sidestepping) and hold its head up. The mouth should remain closed (the dog should not pant).

In no case, should the dog sit or lie down. If your four-legged friend goes along with this, praise it generously and reward it with a treat. This way, after a short time, the dog will confidently put up with standing calmly and properly on the table. You should sign up for a show only when this exercise works well at home.

• Check with local clubs about ring training. Dog show professionals can show you how to use some simple tricks to get your Frenchy to stand properly in the ring or on the judging table.

You will also find out how to move in the ring: in no case, should you saunter slowly around the ring. In some cases, the competitors

This handsome male clearly has show experience.

jog through it. The judge can form a first impression of the dog's gait only at a quick pace (but not jogging).

Also, with ring training, you will find out what the individual evaluation formulas on the judging form mean.

• Get a thin show leash made of leather or nylon—preferably in a color that matches the dog. It should be about 3 feet (1 m) long and have a loop on one end that can be adjusted with a small eyelet so that the dog's head fits through it and yet tightens so that the dog cannot give you the slip in the ring. Alternatively, you can use a narrow metal choke chain and a thin leash.

The Show

On the day of the show, you will get your show number at the ring to which you are directed by the judging program; the number is to be slipped on to your left upper arm so that it is clearly visible, and you wait until your class and show number are called.

Then proceed to the ring, get into order among the other participants according to your starting number, and follow the instructions from the judge.

Generally, all the exhibitors walk a large circle together. Maintain sufficient distance from the person in front of you. The dog is always led on your left side so that you do not block the view of the judge.

Now wait until your dog is called for individual judging. Once again, the judge will invite you to walk with your French Bulldog. The dog must not pull on the leash, lag behind, or bite the leash.

Finally, the dog must show its best side on the judging table just as you have previously trained it to do. Playing, sitting, and lying down have no place in the ring. In no case should you attract the dog's attention with a toy or get any help from a second person outside the show ring. In professional jargon, this is known as *double handling*, and in the worst case it can lead to disqualification.

This is how to present in the show ring: the person is neatly dressed, and the dog runs freely and attentively on the left side.

THE HEALTHY FRENCHY

Of course, the main thing your French Bulldog wants is for you to have enough time for playing and going for walks together. To keep her feeling fine overall, she also needs a healthful diet and daily grooming.

Proper Nutrition

What your Frenchy eats—and how much—has a decisive effect on its well-being and physical and mental fitness. But your dog's requirements keep changing as the years go by: a Frenchy puppy needs different food than an adolescent dog or a fully grown French Bulldog. In old age, the menu must once again be adapted to the new living conditions. You can get the high-quality manufactured foods that supply the nutrients your dog needs every day in every stage of life in pet shops and from your veterinarian. This complete diet contains meat, grains, and vegetables, plus vitamins and minerals, so you don't need to provide any supplements. Of course, sometimes you can give your dog some natural yogurt or a boiled potato. But that should not turn into a habit, or your dog will become picky and its usual food will lose its appeal. If you are not sure what your dog's nutritional requirements are, your breeder and your veterinarian will give you help and advice.

What Frenchies Eat

Dry or wet food? Two or three times a day? Before or after going for a walk? There are several things to keep in mind when it comes to food. But you will know right away if you are doing things right: your dog will enjoy play and exercise, take care of its business two to three times a day, and have a shiny, smooth coat.

Frenchies are real gourmands. And who can resist a wistful look like this? But you must be sure that your dog gets a healthful, balanced diet.

If you have a cat, it will be impossible to keep your Frenchy from occasionally eating its food. As an exceptional case, this doesn't matter much; but it shouldn't be a regular practice. Cat food is very high in protein, and the dog will react to a concentrated load of protein with diarrhea and abdominal bloating—and will become fat.

A Puppy's Diet

For the first six months, a puppy is given three fairly small portions of dry food per day. As for the portion size, you generally can rely on the manufacturer's recommendation on the packaging; if you are not sure, get some advice from your breeder or veterinarian. It's also a good idea to stick to regular feeding times. If your dog has not eaten everything after about 20 minutes, take the dish away and discard the leftovers. In the first place the food goes bad fairly quickly, and in the second you will train the dog to overeat if she always has access to food.

Right after eating the puppy must immediately go outdoors so it can do its business. This consistent daily structure helps the dog become housetrained as quickly as possible.

Since a puppy's stomach is still sensitive, you should always give it the same food that it got in its first home, at least in the first days and weeks. The breeder almost always gives the new owners a bag of the food or tells them where they can buy it. When you go to pick the puppy up, you should also ask about a feeding plan showing when the puppy has been fed and what it likes to eat.

High-quality dog food contains lots of important minerals; feeding this food will encourage the growth of tendons, ligaments, and joints. Better yet consult your veterinarian: he or she can tell you what your little dog really needs, plus he or she probably also sells some excellent food supplements that work best in small amounts. Of course, you can also ask your breeder what body-building products have already shown good results or which products he or she feeds his or her own dogs, and then continue using these foods. Always stick to the breeder's or veterinarian's recommendations. Too much mineral content can lead to stress and hyperactivity, impairments in the growth of the skeleton and the musculoskeletal system, or stomach and intestinal problems and allergies. When you give minerals and food supplements, always observe your dog's behavior very

"Treat." With the help of this magic word, most French Bulldogs are prepared to do anything. But reward them only for good reason and in small morsels. Otherwise, the dog will quickly become too fat.

closely—and be sure to consult your veterinarian if your little friend acts differently.

Young Dog

After about a year, you can switch over from puppy chow to normal dog food for adult dogs. Now you can divide the daily ration into two meals; as for the amount, continue to follow the manufacturer's instructions, as long as your breeder or veterinarian has not prescribed anything different. Also, keep feeding body-building supplements, for French Bulldogs are late bloomers and grow for a long time. They also need additional minerals.

Adult Dog

A healthy adult French Bulldog eats twice a day. It's best to wait until after going on a walk to feed it. After eating, the dog should not be too active; there is a risk of gastric torsion, which can kill your Frenchy if it is not treated right away. For the same reason, you should not play with the dog right after a meal; it's better to let your friend take a rest.

Take away the adult dog's food dish after about 20 minutes if it hasn't yet eaten everything by then. On the other hand, your dog's water dish must always be filled with fresh water at room temperature.

Weight control begins as early as puppyhood. Overfed dogs often have problems with connective tissue and bones (top). Body-building supplements in the form of powders, pills, and pastes are readily accepted—even as a reward, as shown here (bottom).

Senior Dogs

Older French Bulldogs tend to become overweight, as do senior dogs of many other breeds. When your four-legged friend shows the first signs of age, you should switch over to special senior food.

Wet or Dry Food?

Sooner or later, every dog owner is confronted with deciding between wet and dry food. Even though wet food tastes great to Frenchies and often is accepted more readily than dry food by picky eaters, a healthy adult Frenchy should get more dry food. An ideal mix is two-thirds dry food and one third wet, always well mixed.

The reason: wet food often tempts French Bulldogs to gulp, and the result is an upset stomach. Plus the droppings of animals fed with wet food are softer and larger than with dry food, meaning it is not being processed as completely. Dogs that are fed dry food usually have a firmer stool and—as experience shows—significantly less bloating.

Since dry food swells to its ultimate volume in contact with moisture inside the dog's stomach, it keeps the dog feeling full longer and prevents hunger and snack attacks. The chewing process with fairly large dry kibbles also promotes the abrasion of dental tartar. Whatever dog food you choose, make sure it is always at room temperature.

Treats and Other Rewards

You should always keep small treats within reach. They certainly are not necessary for complete nutrition, but they are very helpful in training.

Distribute the treats sparingly; they must not be used as a basic food resource, but really as a reward when the dog does something right or has behaved itself.

Because of the shape of their jaws, French Bulldogs quickly build up dental tartar. Occasionally, you should give your dog a hard roll to chew, or a large boiled beef bone or chew bone to gnaw on a regular or even a daily basis.

But provide chew bones only under supervision. Because Frenchies like to swallow things whole, a piece of the bone could get stuck in the throat, which could lead to a dangerous situation. For the same reason, don't give the dog any small chew bones, poultry bones, or small pork or beef ears.

No Begging

Avoid feeding your French Bulldog from the table. Our food is inappropriate for dogs, and your dog will get in the habit of begging. The things you let your dog get away with at home can quickly become annoying in a park, for instance. You can't expect a dog to distinguish between home and a public place.

Overweight Frenchies

In very rare cases, overweight is a symptom of a serious illness. Generally, food that is too high in calories or fat content is responsible for the Frenchy's excess padding. If your dog is frequently fed from the table and gets too little exercise, it will put on weight. Overweight is not just an appearance problem. The fatter the dog, the greater the likelihood of health problems. It becomes harder to breathe (leading to shortness of breath), the bone structure changes, the liver becomes fatty, and diabetes and heart and circulatory system disorders are the result. All this reduces your dog's life expectancy.

For your dog to live a long, healthy life you should assure that it stays at an appropriate weight through adequate exercise and healthful nutrition. At the proper weight, your Frenchy's waist should be clearly visible from above, and its ribs should be easy to feel.

Your dog is considered significantly overweight, if he or she is more than 15 percent heavier than the normal weight based on size and sex (approximately 18–31 pounds/8–14 kg).

How Do I Keep the Frenchy on a Diet?

Do you feel that your Frenchy is too fat and needs to shed a few pounds? Before you put your dog on a diet, you should consult your veterinarian. Usually, he or she will simply recommend a low-fat diet food to be given according to the guidelines. Between-meals snacks, the occasional potato, and noodles from a plate are then off-limits. If you still want to give your Frenchy a little snack, give it something like a big peeled carrot. As with people, low-calorie food, especially in combination with plenty of exercise, helps with weight loss. Walking on the leash will help you reach your goal more quickly.

Keep an eye on your Frenchy's weight. Love handles are really a drag in the summer.

Care and Prevention

Like all dogs, French Bulldogs need a certain amount of care to keep them healthy and handsome. The dogs take care of some of this themselves—for example, by licking their coats, rubbing their paws over their faces, or shaking to remove water or dirt from their coats. But for everything else, they need help from their humans. Don't worry: you don't need to set aside lots of time, and the grooming program nearly always fits right into the daily petting. Get the puppy used to this early on so it lets you check it over.

Playing with your puppy every day offers a good opportunity to practice. Simply build in a brief break and wait for the puppy to calm down a bit. Now you can start to carefully feel your dog's legs and belly. Gently turn it onto its back during this process, or open its mouth to check its teeth. Don't stop if the dog objects. Be patient, and praise and reward it generously—then later on, the dog will have no problems with the brush and other items. If you associate this exercise with a command right from the beginning, such as "show me your teeth" or "checkup," your dog will know what's expected of it later on during a visit to the veterinarian.

Grooming

In contrast to many other companion dog breeds that have long hair, French Bulldogs have moderate grooming requirements. The short Frenchy coat requires neither hours of combing nor regular washing—leaving more time for cuddling and playing.

To clean the Frenchy's eyes, carefully wipe away from the nose with a soft cloth moistened with lukewarm water.

No Frenchy likes to get its face washed, so start grooming the many facial folds in puppyhood; this will keep you from having a grumpy dog later on.

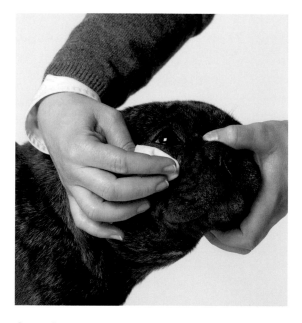

Coat Care

Normally, it's perfectly adequate to "brush" the Frenchy once or twice a week with a soft, rubber glove from the pet shop. It's a good idea to brush a little more often during shedding time in the spring and fall; that way, you leave less hair around the house.

Little white skin scales, which are merely an appearance problem, are quickly removed by rubbing the dog's back with a microfiber dust cloth. This is just as pleasant for the dog as being petted.

Bathing

Bulldogs can be bathed regularly, especially if they smell too doggie or if they have wallowed in some filth, which Frenchies like to do. Since the pH of dog skin is different from that of human skin, you should not use your own shampoo; instead, use a special moisturizing dog shampoo. Also, most "normal" shampoos are scented; they smell nice to us but are a real annoyance to the dog.

For bathing, place the dog into the bathtub or the shower and first rinse its whole body with lukewarm water. Then shampoo the fur thoroughly from front to back. Be sure to keep the shampoo out of the ears, eyes, and nose. It's best to simply clean the head with a damp washcloth. Then carefully rinse everything off with warm water; no traces of shampoo should remain in the coat.

Once the dog shakes the water off its coat, lift the dog out and rub it dry with a towel. Most Frenchies like this part of the bath best, and grunt with pleasure. In warm weather, the toweling is adequate as long as the dog is not exposed to draft. Otherwise blow-dry the fur all the way down to the skin. In the winter or in cooler weather, it's a good idea to do the bathing in the evening so the dog doesn't need to go outdoors again, where she could be stressed by cold weather.

The little French dogs love being brushed and combed. Usually, they purr with delight, like a cat.

To make the bathing process fairly relaxed for all participants, start practicing while the dog is still a puppy: bathe the tiny paws in the shower and give your dog lots of praise when it submits to everything. If you can't avoid it—for example, if the dog has rolled in some filth while playing—you must use a special puppy shampoo from a pet shop. Puppy hair naturally has a higher oil content than the fur of adult dogs, and the oil forms a special protective layer.

Eye Care
Check your French Bulldog's eyes daily for redness, discharge, and injuries. This "examination"

can be done very casually if you pet and snuggle with the dog in a calm moment. If you discover anything noticeable in the process, you should not hesitate to get advice from the veterinarian so that your dog gets the right treatment and necessary medications.

Grooming the Wrinkles on the Frenchy's Head
Just as with the eyes, the wrinkles on the Frenchy's face should be cleaned every day with a soft, moist cloth or with a damp baby wipe (no oily wipes, though). In so doing, stroke each wrinkle in a direction away from the eyes so you don't accidentally force dirt particles or

115

Summertime is bathtime. French Bulldogs love to splash in the water or play with the lawn sprinkler. Despite the hot temperatures, you should thoroughly dry the dog off at the end: with its short coat, it can be stressed by the cold.

small hairs into the eye. Since the wrinkles are not exposed to much air, you must also dry them carefully with a soft cloth to prevent infections.

Keeping the wrinkles clean is especially important with pieds; otherwise, unsightly reddish-brown colorations from the discharge from the eyes builds up on the facial hairs, and they are very difficult to remove.

Ear Care

You should clean your dog's ears once a week. Normally, a French Bulldog moves ear dirt to the outside by shaking its head. The dark ear wax then lodges in the upper part of the outer ear, where it can easily be removed with a tissue or a moist baby wipe (but no oily wipes). At the veterinarian's or a pet shop, you can get solutions in bottles shaped in such a way that they cannot be inserted too deeply in the auditory canal when you administer the drops.

Never attempt to clean the bat ears with cotton swabs. There is a great danger of injuring the inner ear, for the Frenchy might suddenly shake or run away.

Nose Care

Since French Bulldogs cannot lick their noses, they can become chapped. In this case, it is helpful to rub in a little bit of petroleum jelly or baby oil.

Nail Care

A Frenchy's nails should be short and thick. If your dog regularly walks on a hard surface (e.g., paved streets), the nails wear down naturally. Otherwise, you will have to trim them with a special dog nail clipper. But don't cut them too short, because there are blood vessels in the nails. If these are damaged, the dog will bleed a lot.

When the dog gets her second immunization as a puppy, it's a good idea to have the veterinarian show you how to do this and what to watch for. Then you will have no problems later on.

If the dog does not want you to handle her paws or will not hold them still while you trim the nails, it's a good idea to have another person help you: while one holds the Frenchy, the other carefully clips the nails.

Paw Care

Check your dog's paws at regular intervals to see if it has stepped on any foreign object; also check between the toes. If you can't find anything, even though your dog is walking abnormally, you should consult the veterinarian. Also, if there is any redness between the toes (and the Frenchy constantly licks its toes and paws), you should consult with the veterinarian to find out if there is a rash or something similar.

Special paw creams from pet shops are good for paw care. Apply them after going for a

There is nothing more beautiful than owning a fun-loving, healthy Frenchy that is always in the mood to play. Truly healthy dogs are the only ones that should be entered in dog shows.

walk—or better yet, before bedtime; that way, the dog won't spread them all over the house.

Teeth

French Bulldogs are more prone to dental tartar than other dogs, because they like to gulp their food instead of chewing it. If the tartar is not treated, it can lead to serious gum infections; in the worst case, the dog can also lose teeth. To keep that from happening, your Frenchy should chew regularly on a rawhide bone.

Also, have your dog's mouth checked at every regular visit to the veterinarian. A special tooth gel from a pet shop can help prevent dental tartar and infections.

Put some into the dog's mouth with your finger morning and evening after feeding, or if the dog allows, squeeze it directly out of the tube.

If your dog suffers from gum infections, bad breath, or very yellow teeth, a veterinarian can remove tartar from healthy, fairly young dogs under anesthetic (this may cost more than $100). In order for this procedure to be worth it, you should make perfectly sure that the tartar doesn't form again. Take the tips on oral care to heart, and change the dog's food if necessary.

The Frenchy in the Summer

Just as with us humans, the summer is the nicest season for French Bulldogs. As soon as the temperatures rise, the dogs love to take sunbaths.

These bundles of energy love to play in the snow. At the end, you should always dry your Frenchy off well to keep her from feeling the cold.

Every Frenchy owner knows full well how difficult it is to get the dog to choose a shady spot. As with all sun worshippers, if you don't pay attention, the dog can easily experience heatstroke. The first warning signs and symptoms are increased panting and drooling, and sometimes vomiting and diarrhea; thoughts turn to heatstroke also when the dog exhibits irregular movements and staggers. In this case, play it safe and take your Frenchy's temperature. If the thermometer climbs above 104°F (40°C), there is a danger of circulatory collapse.

In extreme heat, it certainly is not advisable to walk with a French Bulldog for fairly long distances. To keep from shortchanging walks and playtime activities in the summer, you should reschedule them for the early morning hours and the evening. If you are in an awkward situation where you have to travel with the dog during the day, you should always have a small bowl and fresh water available; even a moist hand towel can be useful in keeping the dog cool.

Never leave your Frenchy in the car in the summer. Even if the windows are open, the car will heat up inside in no time at all. And since the sun moves quickly, even a shady spot is no guarantee. Under these conditions, it is better to leave your dog home or ask friends to take care of it.

The Frenchy in Winter

Like all dogs, French Bulldogs love to romp in the snow in the winter, chase snowballs, or catch snowflakes. The bad weather in no way dampens their joy in going for a walk. You also needn't fear that your dog will freeze with its short fur. An adult Frenchy generally has adequate defenses, and probably a little fat insulation, to get it through the cold season in good health and cheer.

But it would also be untrue to say that French Bulldogs never suffer from the cold. Because they have no insulating coat and their stomach is not covered with thick hair, they have a tendency to shiver. Going for a walk and romping around is one thing; standing idle in the cold while, for example, you chat with a neighbor, is another. If your dog doesn't move around, it soon will feel the cold and begin to shiver. If you don't move along right away, you are setting the dog up for a chill.

If the weather is wet, rub your dog dry with a hand towel after the walk or blow it dry with a hair dryer (on the lowest setting). Don't forget the paws: it's easy for little clumps of snow, pebbles, and salt particles to get lodged between the toes and cause discomfort. Also, eczema and inflammations can occur easily in the dampness. Then, red spots or even sores appear between the toes and the pads; the dog keeps licking the paws intently. If it is very bad, the dog will begin to limp or hold the paw up. This calls for a quick visit to the veterinarian, for the dog needs treatment with medication.

If you catch your dog eating snow, discourage it with a harsh "Yuck!" The consequence will soon be an upset stomach.

If you are away from home for longer periods during the cold season, you should always have a small blanket and a towel available. When you return to the car, you can use it to towel off the dog.

HEALTH CARE
AND ILLNESSES

Whenever you notice signs of illness or obvious changes in your dog's behavior, you should visit the veterinarian as soon as possible. He or she can make the proper diagnosis and start the appropriate treatment.

A Sick Dog

If you practice with your dog from the time it is little so that strangers can touch every part of its body, palpate it, and look into its mouth, there will be no problems at the veterinarian's. Also before the first real treatment, stop by the clinic a few times so that your dog will not experience any anxiety later on. It will know that nothing bad happens to it there, and it will get a few treats. This helps keep the visit to the veterinarian as stress-free as possible for both human and dog. The veterinarian will show you some exercises you can do at home to train your puppy or young dog for a visit to the doctor. Check on the Internet or at the nearest animal clinic to see if any such practice times are provided.

Regular Health Care

The French Bulldog is no more prone to disease than other dogs. In fact it is extremely robust and doesn't always let on when something is wrong. But if you spend a lot of time with your dog, you will recognize possible ailments and illnesses quite quickly.

The dog needs to be secured in the car even on a trip to the veterinarian.

The practice of arbitrarily vaccinating all puppies on the same schedule is generally obsolete. The age, nutritional status, and health of the puppy, the area where it lives, the prevalent diseases of the region, and exposure potential must all be considered.

Core vaccines are needed by all puppies in most all regions of America. Those vaccines are distemper, infectious hepatitis, parvovirus, and rabies.

Noncore vaccines may be administered to dogs with a higher risk of contracting a specific disease. They include vaccines against parainfluenza, bordetella, leptospirosis, Lyme, giardia, and coronavirus. The need for any or all of those vaccines should be thoroughly discussed with your veterinarian.

Why Vaccinate

The Frenchy dam is vaccinated about the time she is bred. That gives her the greatest possible level of protective antibodies when she whelps. Minimal amounts of those antibodies are transferred to her puppies through intrauterine passage, but most are transferred to the puppies in her colostrum, or "first milk."

This milk is rich in nutrition, but its greatest value is the temporary immunity that her puppies receive from it. Those "passive" antibodies begin diminishing from her puppies almost immediately and are gone within a few weeks.

When to Vaccinate

All puppies should be vaccinated as soon as the natural (passive) immunity has disappeared and before exposure to disease is anticipated. That exact time is virtually impossible to calculate, but veterinary research has found that the protective antibodies of most of the common diseases disappear shortly after natural weaning, or about six weeks of age. At that age, a healthy puppy is very receptive to vaccination and the core vaccines (except rabies) may be given safely and effectively. A booster should be given according to the manufacturer's vaccine-package label or your veterinarian's advice. The rabies vaccine should be administered at six months of age, with a booster at one year. Subsequent core vaccines should be given on an annual basis unless advised to the contrary by your veterinarian.

Your local veterinarian will advise you about noncore vaccine administration. He or she will discuss the occasional reaction to certain vaccines, which diseases are prevalent in your region of the country, and the expected effectiveness of each vaccine.

Canine Distemper (CD) is a viral disease spread by physical contact with an infected dog or by airborne virus particles from coughs and sneezes. Symptoms of CD are loss of appetite, thick yellow or greenish discharge from nose and eyes, lethargy, elevated temperature, muscle tremors, and convulsions. CD often causes

paralysis, and death, and in very young puppies the only sign may be sudden death.

Canine Hepatitis (CAV-1) may mimic distemper and cause sudden death. Its spread is similar to that of distemper, but the virus eventually destroys the liver. Some infected pups will recover but often display cloudy corneas (blue eye) and impaired vision.

Parvovirus is another viral disease that is easily spread by feces and other body discharges from infected dogs. That virus causes high fever, dehydration, heart complications, bloody and copious diarrhea, and vomiting. Sudden death is common. Recovery is possible if supportive therapy is begun quickly, but often various aftereffects remain for life. This virus may live for months in bodily discharges, feces, and contaminated grounds and floors.

Rabies is a fatal viral disease spread through the infected animal's saliva. It may be spread to humans from infected wild animals, livestock, and unvaccinated pets. It is rarely treatable, and usually the infected animal dies before therapy can be considered.

Common Disease Problems

The following illnesses frequently occur in French Bulldogs. With some of them, you can provide first aid yourself. Just the same, you should consult your veterinarian as promptly as possible any time you suspect that something is wrong with your dog or any of the indicated symptoms appear.

A Frenchy's normal body temperature is between 88.7 and 101.3°F (37.5 and 38.5°C). To take the temperature, lubricate a common digital thermometer with petroleum jelly and insert it into the dog's rectum. An elevated or depressed temperature is always a sign that your dog is sick. With dogs that are prone to illness you should always check the temperature.

Anal Sac Blockage

All canines have two anal sacs that empty through pores at the anal opening. Those sacs are lined with glands that secrete a foul fluid onto the dog's feces. If the sacs are not emptied regularly because of the pores being plugged, they become overfilled and cause the dog to scoot on its bottom. If that is unsuccessful, the sacs may become painfully overfilled and infected, causing the dog to lick its anus, look behind itself, and whine. The untreated infected sacs eventually rupture into the anus and will require surgical intervention.

Eye Diseases

The Frenchy's large eyes are susceptible to damage from foreign material lodging in them. That situation causes inflammation, itching, and eventually infection. In that event, the copious tears become thick, the eyes are painful, and the Frenchy wipes the discharge on its feet or the floor. Take your little friend immediately to your veterinarian, who will examine the eyes for foreign material, stain the cornea to diagnose possible ulceration, and probably dispense drops or ointments to treat the infection.

Heatstroke

Frenchies are highly susceptible to heatstroke. That deadly situation is most commonly seen when a Frenchy is left in a car. Heatstroke occurs even when all the windows are down a few inches, the outside temperature is not terribly hot, and skies are cloudy. An automobile's windshield, rear window, and side windows act as magnifiers. The inside of an auto can easily reach 110°F (44°C), and sometimes is recorded above 140°F (60°C).

Signs of heatstroke are rapid respiration, panting, stringy saliva, pale or bluish oral membranes, and unconsciousness. Immediate treatment is necessary. Remove the Frenchy from the car and place it in the shade, cool it with water from a hose, or place it in a tub of water. If your pet responds to first aid, intravenous fluids administered by a veterinarian is the next step. Unfortunately, affected dogs may die before reaching professional help.

Vomiting and Diarrhea

Intestinal upsets are common in puppies and often caused by swallowing indigestible material. Take the Frenchy's temperature, and feel its belly. If the belly is tender and the temperature is elevated more than a degree or two, take the dog to your veterinarian. Conversely, if the vomiting dog has no fever but isn't eating, try withholding all food for 24 hours, allowing small amounts of water frequently. If the dog keeps the water down, after 24 hours give it a small amount of cooked and drained hamburger mixed with equal amounts of cottage cheese and cooked rice. Feed the dog that formula for a day or two and then gradually return normal food to the dog.

Patellar Luxation (dislocation)

In this hereditary condition, the kneecap (patella) leaves its usual position in the stifle (knee) joint. Luxation is caused by genetic weakness of the ligaments of the joint, the groove in which it moves being too shallow, the groove being misaligned, or hereditary deformity of the entire joint.

When the patella leaves its normal position, the Frenchy will walk and run on three legs; after a time the patella may return to its normal location and the dog will look and act normal for a short time. Luxation may be surgically corrected by your veterinarian in most, but not all, cases.

Ear Mites

Those are tiny little parasites that may infest your Frenchy's ear canals. They scurry around on the eardrum and cause frantic itching and the production of thick wax that may be seen exuding from the canal. The inflammation causes the puppy to scratch at the ears and shake its head. Ear-mite infestation is diagnosed by a veterinarian's examination and is easily treated by cleaning the canal and using medicine.

Skin Mites

Skin Mites are microscopic, eight-legged ectoparasites that burrow into the Frenchy's skin and cause serious inflammation, scratching, and

A healthy Frenchy does not need to visit the veterinarian more frequently than other dogs. But if it ever becomes sick, it should approach the waiting room as casually as these two. So far they have had only positive experiences with the doctor.

serum oozing. Diagnosis is made by skin scraping and microscopic mite identification by a veterinarian. Therapy usually is begun with prescription salves, medicated baths, sometimes an injection, and improved nutrition.

Ticks and Fleas
Fleas are part-time tiny residents on the dog. They hop onto your pet from their other residence, the floor of your home, or the lawn. They bite the Frenchy, lapping up the blood that seeps from the bite wound, and hop off again. They often cause a specific dermatitis known as flea-bite allergy. Treating the dog with baths or dips is not terribly effective.

Ticks also live in the dog's environment, but those parasites have two or three hosts. Tick larva are found on one host species, the nymph stage uses a second host, and the final host is your Frenchy. The adult female tick finds a soft spot, often under the dog's collar, and burrows its head under the skin. It sucks blood from the dog until it sometimes reaches the size of a grape. Then the tick mates with a tiny male tick, falls off the dog, and lays thousands of eggs, thus beginning another cycle.

These parasites may transmit various diseases such as tick paralysis, Lyme disease, and tick fever. The parasite may be prevented by medication that is available from your veterinarian. That medicine also may control fleas, heart-worms, and some internal parasites.

Heartworm

This condition is a threat to virtually every dog in America. It is found nationwide and is especially important to short-coated canines such as the French Bulldog. An adult heartworm may reach several inches in length and lives within the dog's heart or its large blood vessels. Heart-worm larvae migrate throughout the infested host's body and into the dog's peripheral vessels, where they are transmitted to a mosquito, which is sucking the blood of the host. The mosquito then sucks the blood of another canine, and the disease is thus spread.

A heavy heartworm infestation may cause cardiac swelling and can compromise the life of your Frenchy. Prevention should be initiated as the veterinarian advises.

Worms

Roundworm, hookworm, and tapeworm are different from one another, and there is no universal therapy for all infestations that is safe and effective. Dogs should never be "wormed" until you are positive that the dog in fact is harboring a parasite infestation.

Roundworm and hookworm infestations are diagnosed and differentiated by a simple, microscopic examination of the feces of the dog.

Tapeworm is a two-host parasite. The adult attaches its head to the intestine of a canine host, and begins to grow to an extreme length, made up of small segments that are loosely hung together. As the tapeworm grows, the segments drop off, pass out of the dog with its feces, and are visible as rice-size, immobile white flecks on the surface of the feces or stuck to the anal hair.

Each segment is composed of a multitude of tiny tapeworm "heads" that are alive but dormant. The segments are thereafter found on blades of grass, and are eaten by a second host, which may vary from a wild herbivorous animal to, in some cases, a flea. The second host is consumed by the dog and the cycle is complete.

What are these five rascals waiting for? Maybe the veterinarian is stopping by with a nice treat.

The Right Veterinarian

A French Bulldog isn't just a dog. You will figure that out by the time you need a good veterinarian. Not all veterinarians are familiar with the specific needs and problems of short-nosed dogs, so it's always worth it to search for the right doctor.

Just as you consult a specialist when you are sick, it is important to find the right doctor for your dog. Look for a clinic where the people are familiar with this breed. Travel farther if you have to, even if your Frenchy only needs to get a shot. It is always advantageous for the veterinarian to be familiar with your pet's "resume."

How to Locate a Good Clinic
It's best to ask your breeder if he or she knows of a good clinic in the area. Even if you live fairly far away, it's worth checking into. Perhaps he or she has already sold a puppy in your area and can say from experience where the nearest animal hospital or veterinary clinic is located. He or she may give you the phone numbers of relevant dog owners so you can contact them and benefit from their past experiences.

If this attempt doesn't work out, you will have to search on your own. First, approach the large clinics. Generally, they have a whole team of veterinarians, so there is a good probability that there is an expert in short-nosed dogs. Ask about a Frenchy specialist—and keep looking if you don't get a positive answer.

If you hit pay dirt, set a time to meet so you can find out what your future veterinarian is

Sun, sand, and muggy air—such things don't bother a healthy Frenchy very much. It gets enough air and has no problems when it pants.

like. Does the doctor approach you and your Frenchy in an open and friendly manner, and are the workers friendly and helpful? Is the clinic clean and neat?

Don't be afraid to ask if other French Bulldogs or other short-nosed dogs are among their patients, such as Griffons and Pugs. If the answer is yes, you have finally found the right veterinarian. Congratulations!

When a Frenchy Grows Old

Through the efforts of responsible breeders, the life expectancy of French Bulldogs has increased significantly in the last 10 years. For a long time 10- or 11-year-old French Bulldogs were exceptional—nowadays this is the average age.

On the day you bring a puppy home you can scarcely conceive that one day the little cutie will become old and frail. Still, you should not distance yourself too much from this realization so that you can provide for old age as much as possible during the dog's youth. The breeders also target their animals' longevity and health through selective breeding.

Until the 1990s most Frenchies died relatively young, for they had some serious problems with such things as intervertebral disc diseases. At that time, many breeders also valued a very short, exaggerated muzzle. But genetic tendencies also play an important role with respect to life expectancy, just as with humans. People who have long-lived ancestors generally live to an old age. It is also because of the good medical treatment and special foods and supplements that today's Frenchies live so long.

When Does a Frenchy Become Old?

As with every living creature, the passage of time affects French Bulldogs. Eventually gray hairs become visible around their muzzles or on their heads. The dog is no longer as active as it once was. Its sleep and nap times become longer, and things that previously were great motivators for your Frenchy—such as the neighbor's cat jumping over the fence, or the humming of the vacuum cleaner—are increasingly accepted without reaction.

Your Frenchy will become increasingly frail, and with the years some little aches and pains will creep in. Bones and joints show the first signs of wear and tear.

The Frenchy "scuffs" with front and hind paws, and when it walks, the hind paws fold under.

You may also notice that your French Bulldog's appetite is no longer what is was, or that it is more selective in eating.

If the dog has tartar on its teeth accompanied by foul breath, they must be cleaned. If the tartar has progressed beyond conservative dentistry and the gums are infected and the teeth loose, they must be extracted. Failure to do so may result in kidney, heart, and other organ damage.

Formerly, anesthetic was a major risk, but today anesthetics are safer and the risk is minimized. Your veterinarian is the person to give advice about lifelong dental care and which products to use.

Gradually switch over from the accustomed food to senior food. These kibbles are not only modified for the specific tooth problems of older dogs, but also have fewer calories.

If you simply keep feeding a French Bulldog the same way as when it was young, it may soon become overweight. And the extra pounds will put even more stress on its already weakened body.

Even in old age, Frenchies are as curious as ever.

To become old and gray with dignity, the Frenchy should remain active into old age. Search games and other exercises also stimulate it mentally. But don't be too lavish with the treats, for your dog will put on weight faster than when it was young.

Use It or Lose It

Older Frenchies still need their daily walks. Checking their "pee-mail" and contact with other dogs keeps them fit. Hide some little treats around the house—for example under plastic flowerpots—and have your dog search for them. That's an appropriate way to stimulate your senior citizen and help keep it fit and agile as long as possible.

Saying Good-bye

Despite the best care, the time will come when your French Bulldog suffers from severe pain. Then it's time to let the dog go. This certainly is one of the most difficult tasks a dog owner faces. But ego and self-interest are just as out of place here as misdirected pity.

Say good-bye. Prove your loyalty to your long-cherished friend by accompanying the dog on its last trip, and don't let it die alone, but in dignity. It is your duty to say *thank you* in this way, for all the time together. When the sadness is over, maybe a little Frenchy puppy will be born somewhere who wants a loyal dog owner like you.

ACKNOWLEDGMENTS

I thank my fellow club members for the hundreds of miles they drove to produce the photos for this book. I wish to thank Barbara Pallasky, Frank Wolter, and Karl Schulze, who provided me with much information on French Bulldogs. Marion and Uli Schädel also deserve mention. They made it possible to picture puppies as young as three weeks old in this book. My friends from Freising, Susi and Peter Seiwert, did the last photo shoot in their house. Finally, I must save a hug for my husband, who was an important motivator in writing this book and has always smiled patiently at my hobby with the fat little dogs.

Susanne Saller-Schneider

Behind the Scenes

Anybody who knows how boisterous, playful, and sometimes hard-headed French Bulldogs are will probably be amazed at the many well-behaved "photo models" in the preceding pages. It was in fact not always easy. But many tireless helpers and even more Frenchies did their best for days on end so that you could form an idea of these wonderful dogs.

While working on this book, I had the good fortune to take part in one of the photo shoots. Since most of the writing takes place at a desk, a day with the main performers is a welcome change of pace.

My photo editor, the photographer, and I were welcomed with open arms to the Seiwerts' home in Freising, along with our own dogs. In

addition to the 15 grown French Bulldogs, there were the brand-new puppy owners from the Seiwert family's most recent litter, along with their 10-week-old protégés. In spite of peak summer temperatures, all the Frenchies showed clearly that they are real purebreds and not to be mistaken for mere fashion accessories. Dogs and owners demonstrated their total

Everybody hold still: lining up seven curious Frenchies for a photo in rank and file is almost more work than herding cats.

So sweet: unfortunately, all the puppies already had new owners.

commitment for more than eight hours that day—and as the wonderful photo gallery shows, it really paid off.

Now there is just one thing left to say: even though I am a professed lover of large dogs, I could not escape being bitten by the Frenchy bug. Once you get used to the backdrop of grunting and snorting and the displays of affection, it really is very easy to lose your heart to these comical French dogs. Nothing steals the show more quickly than a French Bulldog, whether it sits in a studio as a single model or zooms across the fields in a wild pack. The adorable puppies with their giant ears are the only ones that can top the cuteness factor of their parents.

Even the tiniest Frenchy has just as much lust for life, heart, and ego as any of its large cousins. Sooner or later every dog lover will fall for its charm.

Many thanks for the wonderful sensations and encounters to all the Frenchy fans and their dogs!

Regina Denk
Editor

Sometimes you have to use your whole body to get a great photo. Our photographer had to discover firsthand that a Frenchy pup cannot resist this kind of invitation to have a good romp.

AS AN ANIMAL PHOTOGRAPHER, I deal almost daily with dogs and meet the widest variety of breeds and dispositions. For me, Frenchies always embody a bundle of good nature. I quickly got used to standing with my legs apart to keep from losing my balance during the typical Frenchy greeting. It would be a mistake to underestimate these little powerhouses. Fortunately, I have not yet met an unfriendly Frenchy. In shooting the photos for this book it was confirmed repeatedly that the difficulty was not keeping the dogs in the right mood, but rather getting 6 or 8 feet (1.8–2.4 m) away from them so I could just take the photos. The Frenchies would have much preferred to play and romp with me—my usual contortions

in photographing were a perfect invitation to play for the curious little characters. Fortunately, we had plenty of show-seasoned "models" that have been used to standing still ever since they were little.

Naturally, the puppies were less disciplined. But what can you expect from puppies other than looking incredibly sweet—and they certainly did that. And thanks to the devoted breeders, who kept putting the puppies back patiently onto the photo screen after their tenth escape attempt. I was able to take some great photos. The players behind the scenes were just as patient when we could scarcely part from the little imps, for naturally all had found a new family.

So who are you? Fortunately, Frenchies are very curious and keep striking poses as long as you know the right tricks—or get some great help from other animals, as in this photo.

Mrs. Saller-Schneider, who was responsible for the Frenchy casting, could not have performed her duties better. I have never had such a variety of dog models available for a photo project. All together, we photographed around 50 grown Frenchies and 15 puppies, in the most diverse locations all over Germany. The most exceptional shoot was at Mrs. Pallasky's, who summarily employed her parrot to animate the Frenchies. It's only because of this animal support that we managed to get a look at the row of seven French Bulldogs sitting or lying and looking in the same direction. The result is on pages 8 and 9.

If I didn't already have two dogs, I would have reserved at least one puppy from one of the next litters. It is really difficult to resist the charm of these comical fellows.

Heartfelt thanks to all the two- and four-legged participants on and off stage.

Debra Bardowicks
Photographer

Index

Addresses for Further Information

FBDCA (French Bulldog Club of America: the world's oldest Bulldog association, dating from 1897)
frenchbulldogclub.org

French Bulldog Fanciers of Canada (FBFC)
frenchbulldogfanciers.com

French Bulldog Rescue Oregon
frenchbulldog.rescueme.org

Pacific North West French Bulldog Club
pnwfbc.org

French Bulldog Club of Dallas/Fort Worth
frenchietales.com

Eastern Canada French Bulldog Club
frenchbulldogscanada.com

Southeastern French Bulldog Club
sefbdc.com

HOT (Heart of Texas) French Bulldog Club, San Antonio, TX
hotfrenchbulldogclub.com

Chicago French Bulldog Rescue
frenchieporvous.org

Cascade Bulldog Rescue
cascadebulldogrescue.org

French Bulldog Links Directory
Frenchbulldoglinks.com

Great Lakes French Bulldog Club
greatlakesfrenchbulldogclub.com

Mason-Dixon French Bulldog Club
masondixonfrenchbulldogclub.org

Answers to Your Questions About Frenchie Ownership
Consult your local pet shops and veterinarians. You will also find useful information on the computer. Googling *French Bulldogs* will lead you to many useful sites, including the AKC.

Dog Registration
People who wish to protect their dog from animal thieves and death in experimental laboratories can consult veterinarians, pet shops, and computer sites for information on pet registrations.

Helpful Books

Coile, Caroline, Ph.D., *French Bulldogs* (Barron's Complete Pet Owner Manuals). Hauppauge, NY: Barron's, 2005.

The French Bulldog. Vintage Dog Books, 2010.

Dannel, Kathy. *The French Bulldog: An Owner's Guide to a Happy, Healthy Pet.* Howell Book House, 2010.

First edition for the United States, its territories and dependencies, and Canada published in 2012 by Barron's Educational Series, Inc.

First edition translated from the German by Eric A. Bye.

English translation © copyright 2012 by Barron's Educational Series, Inc.

Original title of the book in German is *Französische Bulldogge.*

© Copyright 2011 by Gräfe und Unzer Verlag, GmbH, Munich.

All inquiries should be addressed to:
Barron's Educational Series, Inc.
250 Wireless Boulevard
Hauppauge, New York 11788
www.barronseduc.com

Library of Congress Catalog Card No. 2012002944

ISBN-13: 978-0-7641-6545-0

Library of Congress Cataloging-in-Publication Data
Saller-Schneider, Susanne.
    French bulldogs / Susanne Saller-Schneider.
        p. cm. — (Breed profiles series)
    Includes bibliographical references and index.
    ISBN 978-0-7641-6545-0 (hardback)
    1. French bulldogs. I. Title.
    SF429.F8S25 2012
    636.72—dc23   2012002944

Printed in China
9 8 7 6 5 4 3 2 1